DANIEL BLUM'S

SCREEN WORLD.

1953

BIBLO and TANNEN
NEW YORK

© 1953 by Daniel Blum. Reprinted 1969 by
Biblo & Tannen Booksellers & Publishers, Inc.
63 Fourth Avenue   New York, N.Y. 10003
by arrangement with Crown Publishers, Inc.
Library of Congress Catalogue Card No. 70-84068
Printed in the U.S.A. by Noble Offset Printers, Inc.

TO

HARRIET PARSONS

My Favorite Producer

and

A Loyal Friend

CONTENTS

Title Page Photo: Shirley Booth in
"Come Back, Little Sheba" 4

Film Releases: January 1 to December 31, 1952 8

Portrait Dolls 147

Foreign Films 148

Promising Personalities 163

Obituaries 176

Former Famous Film Folk 178

Index 179

Editorial Assistant: John Willis
Staff Photographers: Constantine, Louis Melancon

Cornel Wilde

Susan Hayward

James Stewart

Virginia Mayo

Hildegarde Neff

Charlton Heston

June Haver

Steve Cochran

Gary Cooper

Katharine Hepburn

James Mason

Joan Crawford

Terry Moore

Fernando Lamas

Gene Tierney

Gilbert Roland

Jerry Lewis

Mitzi Gaynor

Dale Robertson

Linda Darnell

Deborah Kerr

Gene Nelson

Rita Hayworth

Humphrey Bogart

1952 RELEASES

Charles Boyer

Dorothy Lamour

Robert Mitchum

Patrice Wymore

Scott Brady, Jeanne Crain, Thelma Ritter

(20th CENTURY-FOX)

THE MODEL AND THE MARRIAGE BROKER

Producer, Charles Brackett; Director, George Cukor; Screenplay by Charles Brackett, Walter Reisch and Richard Breen; Music by Cyril Mockridge.

CAST

Kitty	Jeanne Crain
Matt	Scott Brady
Mae Swazey	Thelma Ritter
Wixted	Zero Mostel
Doberman	Michael O'Shea
Emmy	Helen Ford
Johannson	Frank Fontaine
Mrs. Gingras	Dennie Moore
Mr. Perry	John Alexander
Chancellor	Jay C. Flippen

and Nancy Kulp, Bunny Bishop, Kathryn Card, Maude Prickett, Athalie Daniell, Dennis Ross, Ken Christy, Shirley Mills, Eve March, Tommy Noonan, Jacqueline French, Edna May Wonacott, June Hedin.

Michael O'Shea, Dennie Moore, Thelma Ritter

Thelma Ritter, Scott Brady, Jeanne Crain

8

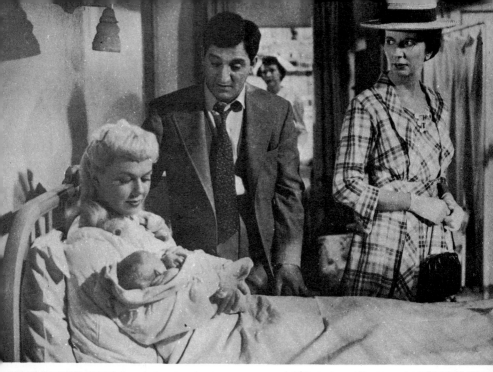

Doris Day, Danny Thomas, Mary Wickes

Doris Day, Danny Thomas

(WARNER BROS.)

I'LL SEE YOU IN MY DREAMS

Producer, Louis F. Edelman; Director, Michael Curtiz; Screenplay by Melville Shavelson and Jack Rose; Songs by Gus Kahn.

CAST

Grace LeBoy Kahn	Doris Day
Gus Kahn	Danny Thomas
Walter Donaldson	Frank Lovejoy
Gloria Knight	Patrice Wymore
Fred Thompson	James Gleason
Anna	Mary Wickes
Johnny Martin	Julie Oshins
Sam Harris	Jim Backus
Mrs. LeBoy	Minna Gombell
Mr. LeBoy	Harry Antrim
Florenz Ziegfeld	William Forrest
Irene (at 6)	Bunny Lewbel
Donald (at 8)	Robert Lyden
Irene (at 3)	Mimi Gibson
Donald (at 4)	Christy Olson

Patrice Wymore and Chorus

9

(M-G-M)
IT'S A BIG COUNTRY

Producer, Robert Sisk; Sequences Directed by Richard Thorpe, John Sturges, Charles Vidor, Don Weis, Clarence Brown, William A. Wellman, Don Hartman; Story for Picture by Dore Schary; Stories for Episodes by William Ludwig and Edgar Brooke, Helen Deutsch, Ray Chordes, Isobel Lennart and Claudia Cranston, Allen Rivkin and Lucile Schlossberg, Dorothy Kingsley, Dore Schary, George Wells and Joseph Petracca.

CAST

Mrs. Brian Patrick Riordan	Ethel Barrymore
Sgt. Maxie Klein	Keefe Brasselle
Texas	Gary Cooper
Miss Coleman	Nancy Davis
Adam Burch	Van Johnson
Icarus Zenophon	Gene Kelly
Rosa Szabo	Janet Leigh
Mrs. Wrenley	Marjorie Main
Papa Esposito	Fredric March
Mr. Callaghan	George Murphy
Professor	William Powell
Stefan Szabo	S. Z. Sakall
Sexton	Lewis Stone
Mr. Stacey	James Whitmore
Michael Fisher	Keenan Wynn
Secret Service Man	Leon Ames
Mama Esposito	Angela Clarke
Joseph Esposito	Bobby Hyatt
Sam Szabo	Sharon McManus

Gene Kelly, Janet Leigh
Top: Van Johnson, Lewis Stone
Below: Bobby Hyatt, Angela Clarke,
Fredric March

Below: Bill Welsh, Ethel Barrymore,
Keenan Wynn, George Murphy

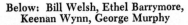

(COLUMBIA)
BOOTS MALONE

Produced and Written by Milton Holmes; Director, William Dieterle; Assistant Director, Milton Feldman; Music by Elmer Bernstein.

CAST

Boots Malone	William Holden
The Kid	Johnny Stewart
Stash Clements	Stanley Clements
Preacher Cole	Basil Ruysdael
John Williams	Carl Benton Reid
Beckett	Ralph Dumke
Howard Whitehead	Ed Begley
Matson	Hugh Sanders
Quarter Horse Henry	Henry Morgan
Mrs. Gibson	Ann Lee
Joe	Anthony Caruso

and Billy Pearson, John W. Frye, Harry Hines, Tony Gerry, Hurley Breen, Whit Bissell, Earl Unkraut, Harry Shannon, John Call.

Stanley Clements, Johnny Stewart,
Basil Ruysdael, William Holden

10

Betsy Drake, Cary Grant, Clifford Tatum, Jr.

WARNER BROS.)

ROOM FOR ONE MORE

Producer, Henry Blanke; Director, Norman
aurog; Assistant Director, Sherry Shourds;
creenplay by Jack Rose and Melville Shavel-
n; Based on Book by Anna Perrott Rose;
usic by Max Steiner.

CAST

Poppy" Rose	Cary Grant
nna Rose	Betsy Drake
iss Kenyon	Lurene Tuttle
rs. Foreman	Randy Stuart
arry Foreman	John Ridgely
ayor	Irving Bacon
rs. Roberts	Mary Lou Treen
ne	Iris Mann
eensie	George Winslow
mmy-John	Clifford Tatum, Jr.
rot	Gay Gordon
im	Malcolm Cassell
en	Larry Olsen

Cary Grant, Betsy Drake

11

(REPUBLIC)

THE WILD BLUE YONDER

Producer, Herbert J. Yates; Director, Allan Dwan; Screenplay by Richard Tregaskis; Story by Andrew Geer and Charles Grayson; Music by Victor Young.

CAST

Capt. Harold Calvert	Wendell Corey
Lt. Helen Landers	Vera Ralston
Maj. Tom West	Forrest Tucker
Sgt. Hank Stack	Phil Harris
Maj. Gen Wolfe	Walter Brennan
Lt. Ted Cranshaw	William Ching
Maj. Ida Winton	Ruth Donnelly
Sgt. Shaker Schuker	Harry Carey, Jr.
Connie Hudson	Penny Edwards
Sgt. Pulaski	Wally Cassell
Sgt. Pop Davis	James Brown
Cpl. Frenchy	Richard Erdman
Sgt. Tony	Phillip Pine
Peanuts	Martin Kilburn
Sgt. O'Hara	Joe Brown, Jr.

and Jack Kelly, Bob Beban, Peter Coe, Hall Bartlett, William Witney, David Sharpe.

Vera Ralston, Wendell Corey

(M-G-M)

THE SELLOUT

Producer, Nicholas Nayfack; Associate Producer, Matthew Rapf; Director, Gerald Mayer; Screenplay by Charles Palmer; Story by Matthew Rapf; Music by David Buttolph.

CAST

Haven Allridge	Walter Pidgeon
Chick Johnson	John Hodiak
Cleo Bethel	Audrey Totter
Peggy Stauton	Paula Raymond
Kellwin Burke	Thomas Gomez
Randy Stauton	Cameron Mitchell
Buck Maxwell	Karl Malden
Nelson Tarsson	Everett Sloane
Ned Grayton	Jonathan Cott
Bennie Amboy	Frank Cady

and Hugh Sanders, Griff Barnett, Burt Mustin, Whit Bissell, Roy Engel, Jeff Richards, Vernon Rich, Bob Stephenson, Cy Stevens.

Cameron Mitchell, Paula Raymond, Walter Pidgeon

(20th-CENTURY FOX)

JAPANESE WAR BRIDE

Producer, Joseph Bernhard; Co-Producer, Anson Bond; Director, King Vidor; Screenplay by Catherine Turney; Story by Anson Bond; Music by Emil Newman, Arthur Lange.

CAST

Tae Shimizu	Shirley Yamaguchi
Jim Sterling	Don Taylor
Art Sterling	Cameron Mitchell
Fran Sterling	Marie Windsor
Ed Sterling	James Bell
Harriet Sterling	Louise Lorimer
Eitaro Shimizu	Philip Ahn
Emily Shafer	Sybil Merritt
Ted Sterling	Orley Lindgren
Woody Blacker	George Wallace

and Lane Nakano, Kathleen Mulqueen, May Takasugi, William Yokota, Susie Matsumoto, Weaver Levy, Jerry Fujikawa, Chieko Sato, Tetsu Komai, Hisa Chiba, David March.

Don Taylor, Shirley Yamaguchi, William Yoko

Buchanan, Forrest Tucker, Sterling Hayden

(PARAMOUNT)
FLAMING FEATHER

Producer, Nat Holt; Associate Producer, Harry Templeton; Director, Ray Enright; Assistant Director, Clarence Eurist; Story and Screenplay by Gerald Drayson Adams; Color by Technicolor; Music by Paul Sawtell.

CAST

Tex McCloud	Sterling Hayden
Lt. Tom Blaine	Forrest Tucker
Nora Logan	Barbara Rush
Carolina	Arleen Whelan
Turquoise	Carol Thurston
Sgt. O'Rourke	Edgar Buchanan
Lucky Lee	Victory Jory
Showdown Calhoun	Richard Arlen
Tombstone Jack	Ian MacDonald
Doc Fallon	George Cleveland
Lafe	Bob Kortman
Ed Poke	Ethan Laidlaw

and Don Dunning, Paul Burns, Ray Teal, Nacho Galindo, Frank Lackteen, Gene Lewis, Larry McGrath, Herman Nowlin, Bryan Hightower, Donald Kerr.

Richard Carlson, Frank Lovejoy

(WARNER BROS.)
RETREAT, HELL!

Producer, Milton Sperling; Director, Joseph H. Lewis; Assistant Director, Oren Haglund; Screenplay by Milton Sperling and Ted Sherdeman; Story by Milton Sperling; Music by William Lava.

CAST

Steve Corbett	Frank Lovejoy
Paul Hansen	Richard Carlson
Jimmy McDermid	Rusty Tamblyn
Ruth Hansen	Anita Louise
Sgt. Novak	Ned Young
Capt. "Tink" O'Grady	Lamont Johnson
"Shorty" Devine	Robert Ellis
Andy Smith	Paul Smith
Maj. Knox	Peter Ortiz
Eve O'Grady	Dorothy Patrick
Capt. Kyser	Mort Thompson
Lt. Ortiz	Joseph Keane

Van Johnson, Dorothy McGuire

(M-G-M)
INVITATION

Producer, Lawrence Weingarten; Director, Gottfried Reinhardt; Screenplay by Paul Osborn; Based on Story by Jerome Weidman; Music by Bronislau Kaper.

CAST

Dan Pierce	Van Johnson
Ellen Pierce	Dorothy McGuire
Maud Redwick	Ruth Roman
Simon Bowker	Louis Calhern
Dr. Warren Pritchard	Ray Collins
Dr. Fromm	Michael Chekhov
Agnes	Lisa Golm
Molly	Diane Cassidy
Gardener	Stapleton Kent
Sarah	Barbara Ruick
Arthur	Norman Field
Paul	Matt Moore
Bill	Patrick Conway
Mr. Redwick	Alex Gerry
Mrs. Redwick	Lucile Curtis

Fredric March, Kevin McCarthy, Don Keefer, Cameron Mitchell
Top: Cameron Mitchell, Mildred Dunnock, Fredric March, Kevin McCarthy

14

(COLUMBIA)
DEATH OF A SALESMAN

Producer, Stanley Kramer; Associate Producer, George Glass; Director, Laslo Benedek; Assistant Director, Frederick Briskin; Screenplay by Stanley Roberts; Based on Play by Arthur Miller; Music by Alex North.

CAST

Willy Loman .... Fredric March
Linda Loman .... Mildred Dunnock
Biff .... Kevin McCarthy
Happy .... Cameron Mitchell
Ben .... Howard Smith
Charley .... Royal Beal
Bernard .... Don Keefer
Stanley .... Jesse White
Miss Francis .... Claire Carleton
Howard Wagner .... David Alpert
Miss Forsythe .... Elizabeth Fraser
Jenny .... Patricia Walker

Mildred Dunnock, Kevin McCarthy
Center: Cameron Mitchell, Kevin McCarthy
Top: Don Keefer, Fredric March

Mildred Dunnock
Top: Fredric March

15

(M-G-M)
THE BELLE OF NEW YORK

Producer, Arthur Freed; Director, Charles Walters; Screenplay by Robert O'Brien and Irving Elinson; Adapted by Chester Erskine; From the Play by Hugh Morton; Music by Harry Warren; Lyrics by Johnny Mercer; Musical Numbers Staged and Directed by Robert Alton; Color by Technicolor.

CAST

Charlie Hill	Fred Astaire
Angela Bonfils	Vera-Ellen
Mrs. Phineas Hill	Marjorie Main
Max Ferris	Keenan Wynn
Elsie Wilkins	Alice Pearce
Gilfred Spivak	Clinton Sundberg
Dixie McCoy	Gale Robbins
Frenchie	Lisa Ferraday
Clancy	Henry Slate
Frenchie's Girls	Carol Brewster, Meredith Leeds, Lyn Wilde
Judkins	Roger Davis
Cab Driver	Buddy Roosevelt
Bowery Bums	Dick Wessel, Percy Helton, Tom Dugan

Fred Astaire, Henry Slate, Keenan Wynn, Dick Wessell, Clinton Sundberg

Vera-Ellen, Fred Astaire

Vera-Ellen, Fred Astaire
Center: Marjorie Main, Vera-Ellen, Alice Pea...

16

Dean Martin, Jerry Lewis

Jerry Lewis, Marion Marshall
Below: Jerry Lewis, Dean Martin

(PARAMOUNT)

SAILOR BEWARE

Producer, Hal B. Wallis; Director, Hal Walker; Screenplay by James Allardice and Martin Rackin; Adaptation by Elwood Ullman; Based on Play by Kenyon Nicholson and Charles Robinson; Songs by Mack David and Jerry Livingston, and Thurston Knudson.

CAST

Al Crowthers	Dean Martin
Melvin Jones	Jerry Lewis
Guest Star	Corinne Calvet
Hilda	Marion Marshall
Lardoski	Robert Strauss
Cmdr. Lane	Leif Erickson
Mr. Chubby	Don Wilson
Blayden	Vincent Edwards
Mac	Skip Homeier
'Bama	Dan Barton
Tiger	Mike Mahoney
Ginger	Mary Treen

Dean Martin, Corinne Calvet, Marion Marshall,
Jerry Lewis

(WARNER BROS.)
THIS WOMAN IS DANGEROUS

Producer, Robert Sisk; Director, Felix Feist; Assistant Director, Russ Saunders; Screenplay by Geoffrey Homes and George Worthing Yates; Based on Story by Bernard Girard; Music by David Buttolph.

CAST

Beth Austin	Joan Crawford
Dr. Ben Halleck	Dennis Morgan
Matt Jackson	David Brian
Franklin	Richard Webb
Ann Jackson	Mari Aldon
Will Jackson	Philip Carey
Joe Crossland	Ian MacDonald
Nurse	Katherine Warren
Ned Shaw	William Challee
Susan	Sherry Jackson
McGill	Stuart Randall
Mike	Harry Tyler

and George Chandler, Douglas Fowley, Kenneth Patterson, Gladys Blake, Cecil Weston.

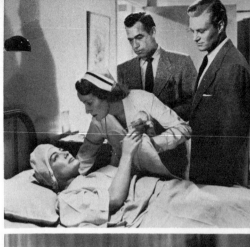

Joan Crawford, Dennis Morgan
Top: Joan Crawford, Katherine Warren, Stuart Randall, Richard Webb
Left: Joan Crawford

(20th CENTURY-FOX)
RED SKIES OF MONTANA*

Producer, Samuel G. Engel; Director, Joseph M. Newman; Screenplay by Harry Kleiner; Based on Story by Art Cohn; Color by Technicolor; Music by Sol Kaplan.

CAST

Cliff Mason	Richard Widmark
Peg	Constance Smith
Ed Miller	Jeffrey Hunter
Dryer	Richard Boone
Steve	Warren Stevens
Boise	James Griffith
Pop Miller	Joe Sawyer
Randy	Gregory Wolcott
Noxon	Richard Crenna
Felton	Bob Nichols
Piney	Ralph Reed
Winkler	William Murphy

and Robert Adler, Charles Buchinsky, Mike Mahoney, Larry Dobkin, John Close, Grady Galloway, Henry Kulky, Harry Carter, Charles Tannen.

*Changed to SMOKE JUMPERS.

Richard Boone, Richard Widmark

18

Warren Stevens, Bette Davis

(20th CENTURY-FOX)

PHONE CALL
FROM A STRANGER

Producer, Nunnally Johnson; Director, Jean Negulesco; Screenplay by Nunnally Johnson; Based on Story by I.A.R. Wylie; Music by Franz Waxman.

CAST

Binky Gay	Shelley Winters
David Trask	Gary Merrill
Dr. Fortness	Michael Rennie
Eddie Hoke	Keenan Wynn
Sally Carr	Evelyn Varden
Marty Nelson	Warren Stevens
Mrs. Fortness	Beatrice Straight
Jerry Fortness	Ted Donaldson
Mike Carr	Craig Stevens
Jane Trask	Helen Westcott
Marie Hoke	Bette Davis

and Sydney Perkins, Hugh Beaumont, Thomas Jackson, Harry Cheshire, Tom Powers, Freeman Lusk, George Eldredge, Nestor Paiva, Perdita Chandler, Genevieve Bell.

Center: Bette Davis, Gary Merrill; Gary Merrill; Shelley Winters
Top: Keenan Wynn, Shelley Winters, Gary Merrill, Michael Rennie

John Lund, Ann Sheridan, Howard Duff

(UNIVERSAL)
STEEL TOWN

Producer, Leonard Goldstein; Associate Producer, Ross Hunter; Director, George Sherman; Screenplay by Gerald Drayson Adams and Lou Breslow; Based on Story by Leonard Freeman.

CAST

"Red McNamara"	Ann Sheridan
Steve Kostane	John Lund
Jim Denko	Howard Duff
Joe	James Best
Millie	Eileen Crowe
Mac	William Harrigan
Ernie	Chick Chandler
Delores	Nancy Kulp

Ralph Meeker, Jean Hagen

(M-G-M)
SHADOW IN THE SKY

Producer, William H. Wright; Director, Fred M. Wilcox; Screenplay by Ben Maddow; Based on Story by Edward Newhouse; Music by Bronislau Kaper.

CAST

Burt	Ralph Meeker
Betty	Nancy Davis
Lou	James Whitmore
Stella	Jean Hagen
Mrs. Lehner	Gladys Hurlbut
Doctor	Eduard Franz
Chris	Dennis Ross
Nina	Nadene Ashdown
Clayton	John Lupton
Doug	Jonathan Cott

Clark Gable, Ava Gardner, Lowell Gilmore, Victor Sutherland

(M-G-M)
LONE STAR

Producer, Z. Wayne Griffin; Director, Vincent Sherman; Screenplay by Borden Chase; Based on Screen Story by Howard Estabrook from the Magazine Story by Borden Chase; Music by David Buttolph.

CAST

Devereaux Burke	Clark Gable
Martha Ronda	Ava Gardner
Thomas Craden	Broderick Crawford
Andrew Jackson	Lionel Barrymore
Minniver Bryan	Beulah Bondi
Claud Demmet	Ed Begley
Luther Kilgore	James Burke
Tom Crockett	William Farnum
Capt. Elliott	Lowell Gilmore
Sam Houston	Moroni Olsen
Maynard Cole	Russell Simpson
Bud Yoakum	Ralph Reed
Ben McCulloch	Jonathan Cott

and William Conrad, Lucius Cook, Ric Roman, Victor Sutherland, Charles Cane, Nacho Galindo, Trevor Bardette, Harry Woods, Dudley Sadler, Emmett Lynn.

(UNIVERSAL)

BEND OF THE RIVER

Producer, Aaron Rosenberg; Director, Anthony Mann; Screenplay by Borden Chase; Based on Novel by Bill Gulick; Color by Technicolor; Music by Hans J. Salter.

CAST

Glyn McLyntock	James Stewart
Emerson Cole	Arthur Kennedy
Laura Baile	Julia Adams
Trey Wilson	Rock Hudson
Jeremy Baile	Jay C. Flippen
Adam	Stepin Fetchit
Marjie	Lori Nelson
Shorty	Henry Morgan
Capt. Mello	Chubby Johnson
Tom Hendricks	Howard Petrie
Mrs. Prentiss	Frances Bavier
Red	Jack Lambert
Long Tom	Royal Dano
Wullie	Cliff Lyon

Julia Adams, Arthur Kennedy, James Stewart
Top: Julia Adams, James Stewart

James Stewart, Arthur Kennedy

Frank Ferguson, Arthur Kennedy, Rock Hudson
Above: Jay C. Flippen, Rock Hudson, Julia Adams

21

Katharine Hepburn, Humphrey Bogart
Top: Humphrey Bogart, Katharine Hepburn

(UNITED ARTISTS)

THE AFRICAN QUEEN

Producer, S. P. Eagle; Director, John Huston; Screenplay by James Agee and John Huston; Based on Novel by C. S. Forester; Color by Technicolor; Music by Allan Gray; A Horizon-Romulus Production.

CAST

Charlie Allnut	Humphrey Bogart
Rose	Katharine Hepburn
Brother	Robert Morley
Captain of Louisa	Peter Bull
1st Officer	Theodore Bikel
2nd Officer	Walter Cotell
Petty Officer	Gerald Onn
1st Officer of Shona	Peter Swanick
2nd Officer of Shona	Richard Marner

Humphrey Bogart, Katharine Hepburn   Katharine Hepburn, Humphrey Bogart
Top: Humphrey Bogart, Katharine Hepburn

23

(20th CENTURY-FOX)
RETURN OF THE TEXAN

Producer, Frank P. Rosenberg; Director, Delmer Daves; Screenplay by Dudley Nichols; Based on Novel by Fred Gipson; Music by Sol Kaplan.

CAST

Sam Crockett	Dale Robertson
Ann Marshall	Joanne Dru
Firth Crockett	Walter Brennan
Rod	Richard Boone
Stud Spiller	Tom Tully
Dr. Harris	Robert Horton
Averill	Helen Westcott
Yo-Yo	Lonnie Thomas
Steve	Dennis Ross
Foreman	Robert Adler
Housekeeper	Kathryn Sheldon
Cordy Spiller	Aileen Carlyle
Spiller Girl	Linda Green
Spiller Boy	Brad Mora

Joanne Dru, Dale Robertson

(COLUMBIA)
OKINAWA

Producer, Wallace MacDonald; Director, Leigh Jason; Screenplay by Jameson Brewer and Arthur Ross; From Story by Arthur Ross; Additional Dialogue by Leonard Stern.

CAST

Lt. Cmdr. Hale	Pat O'Brien
Grip	Cameron Mitchell
Lt. Phillips	Richard Denning
Roberg	Rhys Williams
Emerson	James Dobson
Delagado	Richard Benedict
Felix	Rudy Robles
Lt. Sanders	Don Gibson
Yeoman	George Cooper
Chief Pharmacist Mate	Alan Dreeben
Smith	Norman Budd
Quartermaster	Alvy Moore

Richard Denning, Pat O'Brien, James Dobson Cameron Mitchell

(UNIVERSAL)
FLESH AND FURY

Producer, Leonard Goldstein; Director, Joseph Pevney; Screenplay by Bernard Gordon; Story by William Alland; Music by Hans J. Salter.

CAST

Paul Callan	Tony Curtis
Sonya Bartow	Jan Sterling
Ann Hollis	Mona Freeman
Jack Richardson	Wallace Ford
Mrs. Richardson	Connie Gilchrist
Mrs. Hollis	Katherine Locke
Cliff	Joe Gray
Al Logan	Ron Hargrave
Lou Callan	Harry Guardino
Mike Callan	Harry Shannon
Murph	Harry Raven
Whitey	Ted Stanhope

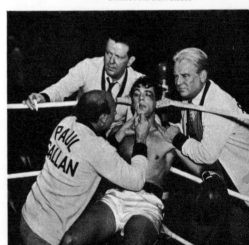

Harry Raven, Tony Curtis, Wallace Ford

rrest Tucker, Ray Milland, Barton MacLane

(WARNER BROS.)

BUGLES IN THE AFTERNOON

Producer, William Cagney; Director, Roy Rowland; Assistant Director, William Kissel; Screenplay by Geoffrey Homes and Harry Brown; Based on Novel by Ernest Haycox; Music by Dimitri Tiomkin; Color by Technicolor.

CAST

Sgt. Kern Shafter	Ray Milland
Josephine Russell	Helena Carter
Capt. Edward Garnett	Hugh Marlowe
Pvt. Donovan	Forrest Tucker
Capt. Myles Moylan	Barton MacLane
Lt. Smith	George Reeves
1st Sgt. Hines	James Millican
May	Gertrude Michael
Bannack Bill	Stuart Randall
Pvt. Tinney	William "Bill" Phillips
Maj. Gen. Custer	Sheb Wooley
Pvt. McDermott	John Pickard

(PARAMOUNT)

SOMETHING TO LIVE FOR

Producer-Director, George Stevens; Associate Producer, Ivan Moffat; Associate Director, Fred Guiol; Screenplay by Dwight Taylor.

CAST

Jenny Carey	Joan Fontaine
Alan Miller	Ray Milland
Edna Miller	Teresa Wright
Tony Collins	Richard Derr
Baker	Douglas Dick
Mr. Crawley	Herbert Heyes
Billy	Harry Bellaver
Albert	Paul Valentine
Waiter	Frank Orth
Young Man	Bob Cornthwaite
Mrs. Crawley	Helen Spring
Chris Miller	Rudy Lee
Johnny Miller	Patric Mitchell

Ray Milland, Joan Fontaine

(M-G-M)

LOVE IS BETTER THAN EVER

Producer, William H. Wright; Director, Stanley Donen; Screenplay by Ruth Brooks Flippen.

CAST

Jud Parker	Larry Parks
Anastacia Macaboy	Elizabeth Taylor
Mrs. Macaboy	Josephine Hutchinson
Mr. Macaboy	Tom Tully
Mrs. Levoy	Ann Doran
Pattie Marie Levoy	Elinor Donohue
Mrs. Kahrney	Kathleen Freeman
Albertina Kahrney	Doreen McCann
Hamlet	Alex Gerry
Smittie	Dick Wessel

and Jack George, Dan Foster.

Larry Parks, Elizabeth Taylor

(20th CENTURY-FOX)

VIVA ZAPATA!

Producer, Darryl F. Zanuck; Director, Elia
Kazan; Screenplay by John Steinbeck; Music
by Alex North.

CAST

Zapata	Marlon Brando
Josefa	Jean Peters
Eufemio	Anthony Quinn
Fernando	Joseph Wiseman
Don Nacio	Arnold Moss
Pancho Villa	Alan Reed
Soldadera	Margo
Madero	Harold Gordon
Pablo	Lou Gilbert
Señora Espejo	Mildred Dunnock
Huerta	Frank Silvera
Aunt	Nina Varela
Señor Espejo	Florenz Ames
Diaz	Fay Roope

and Bernie Gozier, Frank De Kova, Joseph
Granby, Pedro Regas, Richard Garrick, Harry
Kingston, Ross Bagdasarian, Leonard George,
Will Kuluva, Fernanda Eliscu, Abner Biber-
man, Philip Van Zandt, Lisa Fusaro, Belle
Mitchell.

Marlon Brando
Right: Marlon Brando, Jean Peters
Top: Rick Roman, Marlon Brando, Arnold Moss

Anthony Quinn, Marlon Brando, Lou Gilbert, Harold Gordon
Top: Marlon Brando, Jean Peters

(R K O)

RANCHO NOTORIOUS

Producer, Howard Welsch; Director, Fritz Lang; Screenplay by Daniel Taradash; Story by Sylvia Richards; Assistant Director, Emmett Emerson; Music by Emil Newman; Songs by Ken Darby; Color by Technicolor; A Fidelity Pictures Production.

CAST

Altar Keane	Marlene Dietrich
Vern Haskell	Arthur Kennedy
Frenchy Fairmont	Mel Ferrer
Beth	Gloria Henry
Baldy Gunder	William Frawley
Maxine	Lisa Ferraday
Chuck-a-Luck Dealer	John Raven
Geary	Jack Elam
Wilson	George Reeves
Preacher	Frank Ferguson

and Francis McDonald, Dan Seymour, John Kellogg, Rodric Redwing, Stuart Randall, Roger Anderson, Charles Gonzales, Felipe Turich, Jose Dominguez, Stan Jolley, John Doucette.

Arthur Kennedy, Marlene Dietrich

(WARNER BROS.)

THE BIG TREES

Producer, Louis F. Edelman; Director, Felix Feist; Assistant Director, Frank Mattison; Screenplay by John Twist and James R. Webb; Based on Story by Kenneth Earl; Music by Heinz Roemheld; Color by Technicolor.

CAST

Jim Fallon	Kirk Douglas
Alicia Chadwick	Eve Miller
Daisy Fisher	Patrice Wymore
Yukon Burns	Edgar Buchanan
"Frenchy" LeCroix	John Archer
"Tiny"	Alan Hale, Jr.
Judge Crenshaw	Roy Roberts
Elder Bixby	Charles Meredith
Cleve Gregg	Harry Cording
Mrs. Blackburn	Ellen Corby

Kirk Douglas, Patrice Wymore

Eve Miller, Kirk Douglas

Millard Mitchell   Alf Kjellin   Gilbert Roland   Marshall Thompson

Marshall Thompson, Henry Morgan, Gilbert Roland, John Beal, Alf Kjellin, Millard Mitchell, Jay Adler

(COLUMBIA)

MY SIX CONVICTS

Producer, Stanley Kramer; Associate Producers, Edna and Edward Anhalt; Director, Hugo Fregonese; Screenplay by Michael Blankfort; Based on Book by Donald Powell Wilson; Music by Dimitri Tiomkin; Assistant Director, James Casey.

CAST

James Connie	Millard Mitchell
Punch Pinero	Gilbert Roland
Doc	John Beal
Blivens Scott	Marshall Thompson
Clem Randall	Alf Kjellin
Dawson	Henry Morgan
Steve Kopac	Jay Adler
Dr. Gordon	Regis Toomey
Warden Potter	Fay Roope
Capt. Haggerty	Carleton Young
Knotty Johnson	John Marley
Dr. Hughes	Russ Conway
Doc Brint	Byron Foulger
Higgins	Jack Carr
Mrs. Randall	Carol Savage

Left: John Beal, Gilbert Roland

(20th CENTURY-FOX)

FIVE FINGERS

Producer, Otto Lang; Director, Joseph L. Mankiewicz; Screenplay by Michael Wilson; Based on Novel by L. C. Moyzisch; Music by Bernard Herrmann.

CAST

Cicero	James Mason
Anna	Danielle Darrieux
George Travers	Michael Rennie
Sir Frederic	Walter Hampden
Moyzisch	Oscar Karlweis
Col. von Richter	Herbert Berghof
Von Papen	John Wengraf
Siebert	A. Ben Astar
MacFadden	Roger Plowden
Morrison	Michael Pate
Steuben	Ivan Triesault

and Hannelore Axman, David Wolfe, Larry Dobkin, Nestor Paiva, Antonio Filauri, Richard Loo.

James Mason, Danielle Darrieux
Top: Walter Hampden, James Mason, Michael Rennie

James Mason, Oscar Karlweis

30

Oscar Karlweis, Herbert Berghof,
Danielle Darrieux
Center: Walter Hampden, James Mason

James Mason
Top: James Mason, Danielle Darrieux

31

Helen Hayes

(PARAMOUNT)

MY SON, JOHN

Producer-Director, Leo McCarey; Screenplay by Myles Conolly and Leo McCarey; Adapted by John Lee Mahin; Story by Leo McCarey; Music by Robert Emmett Dolan.

CAST

Lucille Jefferson	Helen Hayes
John Jefferson	Robert Walker
Mr. Stedman	Van Heflin
Dan Jefferson	Dean Jagger
Dr. Carver	Minor Watson
Father O'Dowd	Frank McHugh

Percy Kilbride, Marjorie Main

(UNIVERSAL)

MA AND PA KETTLE
AT THE FAIR

Producer, Leonard Goldstein, Direc
Charles Barton; Screenplay by Richard Mo
and John Grant; Story by Martin Ragaw
Leonard Stern and Jack Henley; Music
Joseph Gershenson.

CAST

Ma Kettle	Marjorie M
Pa Kettle	Percy Kilbr
Marvin Johnson	James B
Rosie Kettle	Lori Nels
Birdie Hicks	Esther D
Billy Reed	Emory Parr
Geoduck	Oliver Bla
Crowbar	Zachary Char
Clem Johnson	Russell Simps
Sheriff	Rex Le

Wendell Corey, Stewart Granger, Cyd Charisse

(M-G-M)

THE WILD NORTH

Producer, Stephen Ames; Director, Andr
Marton; Screenplay by Frank Fenton; Music
Bronislau Kaper; Photographed in Ansco Col

CAST

Jules Vincent	Stewart Gran
Constable Pedley	Wendell Co
Indian Girl	Cyd Chari
Father Simon	Morgan Far
Callahan	J. M. Kerrig
Brody	Howard Pet
Old Man	Houseley Stevens
Sergeant	Lewis Mar
Indian Chief	John War Ea
Ruger	Ray T
Sloan	Clancy Coo

(RKO)

MACAO

Producer, Alex Gottlieb; Director, Josef von Sternberg; Screenplay by Bernard C. Schoenfeld and Stanley Rubin; From a Story by Bob Williams; Songs by Johnny Mercer, Harold Arlen, Jule Styne and Leo Robin; Music by Anthony Collins.

CAST

Nick Cochran	Robert Mitchum
Julie Benson	Jane Russell
Lawrence Trumble	William Bendix
Lt. Sebastian	Thomas Gomez
Margie	Gloria Grahame
Halloran	Brad Dexter
Martin Stewart	Edward Ashley
Itzumi	Philip Ahn
Kwan Sum Tang	Vladimir Sokoloff
Gimpy	Don Zelaya

Robert Mitchum, Jane Russell

(M-G-M)

JUST THIS ONCE

Producer, Henry Berman; Director, Don Weis; Screenplay by Sidney Sheldon; Based on Story by Max Trell; Music by David Rose.

CAST

Lucy Duncan	Janet Leigh
Mark MacLene	Peter Lawford
Judge Samuel Coulter	Lewis Stone
Gertrude Crome	Marilyn Erskine
Tom Winters	Richard Anderson
Frank Pirosh	Douglas Fowley
Mr. Blackwell	Hanley Stafford
Jeff Parma	Henry Slate
Stanley Worth	Jerry Hausner
Herbert Engel	Benny Rubin
Adam Backwith	Charles Watts

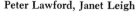

Peter Lawford, Janet Leigh

(PARAMOUNT)

AARON SLICK
FROM PUNKIN CRICK

Producers, William Perlberg and George Seaton; Director, Claude Binyon; Screenplay by Claude Binyon; Based on Play by Walter Benjamin Hare; Color by Technicolor; Music and Lyrics by Jay Livingston and Ray Evans; Musical Numbers Staged by Charles O'Curran.

CAST

Aaron Slick	Alan Young
Josie Berry	Dinah Shore
Bill Merridew	Robert Merrill
Gladys	Adele Jergens
Mrs. Peabody	Minerva Urecal
Soubrette	Martha Stewart
Headwaiter	Fritz Feld
Girl in Red	Veda Ann Borg
Watchman	Chick Chandler

Alan Young, Robert Merrill, Adele Jergens

TALK ABOUT A STRANGER

Producer, Richard Goldstone; Director, David Bradley; Screenplay by Margaret Fitts; Based on Story by Charlotte Armstrong; Music by David Buttolph; Associate Producer, Sol Baer Fielding.

CAST

Robert Fontaine, Sr.	George Murphy
Marge Fontaine	Nancy Davis
Robert Fontaine, Jr.	Billy Gray
Mr. Wardlaw	Lewis Stone
Matlock	Kurt Kasznar
Camille Wardlaw	Anna Glomb

and Tudor Owen, Katharine Warren, Stanley Andrews, Harry Hinds, Les O'Pace, Bill Tannen, Ed Cassidy, Mitchell Lewis.

Billy Gray, Nancy Davis, George Murphy
Left: Kurt Kasznar, Billy Gray

(M-G-M)

WHEN IN ROME

Producer and Director, Clarence Brown; Screenplay by Charles Schnee and Dorothy Kingsley; Based on Story by Robert Buckner; Music by Carmen Dragon.

CAST

Father John	Van Johnson
Joe Brewster	Paul Douglas
Aggiunto Bodulli	Joseph Calleia
Antonio Silesto	Carlo Rizzo
Father McGinniss	Tudor Owen
Commissario, Genoa	Dino Nardi
Cabby	Aldo Silvani
Luigi Lugacetti	Mario Siletti
Mrs. Lugacetti	Argentina Brunetti
Rosa	Mimi Aguglia
Ship's Captain	Emory Parnell

and Charles Fawcett, Alberto Lolli, Adriano Ambrogi, Amina Pirani Maggi, Carlo Borrelli, Giuseppe Pierozzi, Guido Martufi, Joe Faletta.

Van Johnson, Paul Douglas

Van Johnson, Renata Varni, Allan Sharp

(COLUMBIA)
THE MARRYING KIND

Producer, Bert Granet; Director, George Cukor; Screenplay by Ruth Gordon and Garson Kanin; Music by Hugo Friedhofer.

CAST

Florence Keefer	Judy Holliday
Chet Keefer	Aldo Ray
Judge Carroll	Madge Kennedy
Joan Shipley	Sheila Bond
Howard Shipley	John Alexander
George Bastian	Rex Williams
Mrs. Derringer	Phyllis Povah
Emily Bundy	Peggy Cass
Pat Bundy	Mickey Shaughnessy
Charley	Griff Barnett
Ellen	Susan Hallaran
Joey	Barry Curtis and Christie Olsen
Newhouse	Wallace Acton
Marian	Elsie Holmes

Christie Olsen, Judy Holliday, Susan Hallaran, Aldo Ray
Top: Aldo Ray, Judy Holliday

Judy Holliday, Aldo Ray, Rex Williams, Elsie Holmes
Center: Judy Holliday, Madge Kennedy, Aldo Ray

Gene Kelly, Debbie Reynolds

Jean Hagen, Gene Kelly

Top: Donald O'Connor, Debbie Reynolds, Gene Kelly, Jean Hagen, Millard Mitchell

Center: Gene Kelly and Chorus

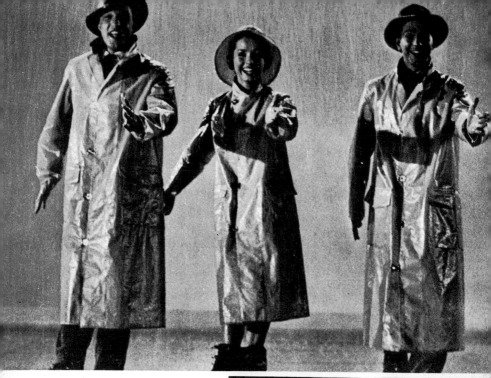

(M-G-M)

SINGIN' IN THE RAIN

Producer, Arthur Freed; Directors, Gene Kelly and Stanley Donen; Story and Screenplay by Adolph Green and Betty Comden; Lyrics by Arthur Freed; Music by Nacio Herb Brown; Color by Technicolor.

CAST

Don Lockwood	Gene Kelly
Cosmo Brown	Donald O'Connor
Kathy Selden	Debbie Reynolds
Lina Lamont	Jean Hagen
R. F. Simpson	Millard Mitchell
Guest Artist	Cyd Charisse
Zelda Zanders	Rita Moreno
Roscoe Dexter	Douglas Fowley
Dora Bailey	Madge Blake

Gene Kelly, Debbie Reynolds
Top: Gene Kelly, Debbie Reynolds,
Donald O'Connor

Debbie Reynolds, Gene Kelly, Jean Hagen

(R K O)

TARZAN'S SAVAGE FURY

Producer, Sol Lesser; Director, Cyril Endfield; Assistant Director, Mack V. Wright; Screenplay by Cyril Hume and Hans Jacoby and Shirley White; Based on characters created by Edgar Rice Burroughs; Music by Paul Sawtell.

CAST

Tarzan	Lex Barker
Jane	Dorothy Hart
Edwards	Patric Knowles
Rokov	Charles Korvin
Joey	Tommy Carlton

Lex Barker, Tommy Carlton
Left: Lex Barker, Dorothy Hart

(20th CENTURY-FOX)

THE PRIDE OF ST. LOUIS

Producer, Jules Schermer; Director, Harmon Jones; Screenplay by Herman J. Mankiewicz, Based on Story by Guy Trosper; Music by Arthur Lange.

CAST

Dizzy Dean	Dan Dailey
Patricia Nash Dean	Joanne Dru
Johnny Kendall	Richard Hylton
Paul Dean	Richard Crenna
Horst	Hugh Sanders
Moose	James Brown
Manager Ed Monroe	Leo T. Cleary
Castleman	Kenny Williams
Delaney	John McKee
Frankie Frisch	Stuart Randall
Herbie	William Frambes
Johnnie Bishop	Damian O'Flynn

and Cliff Clark, Billy Nelson, Pattee Chapman, Richard Reeves, Bob Nichols, John Duncan, Clyde Trumbull, John Butler, Freeman Lusk, Jack Rice, Al Green, Phil Van Zandt, Victor Sutherland, Kathryn Card, George MacDonald, Joan Sudlow, Fred Scannell, Larry Thor, John Wald, Hank Weaver, William Forman, Jack Sherman, Tom Hanlon, Chet Huntley, John Doucette, Harris Brown.

Dan Dailey, Joanne Dru
Right Center: Dan Dailey, Joanne Dru

40

(WARNER BROS.)

JACK AND THE BEANSTALK

Producer, Alex Gottlieb; Director, Jean Yarbrough; Assistant Director, Alfred Westen; Screenplay by Nat Curtis; From a Story by Pat Costello; Music by Heinz Roemheld; Color by Supercinecolor; An Exclusive Productions Picture.

CAST

Dinkelpuss	Bud Abbott
Jack	Lou Costello
Sgt. Riley	Buddy Baer
Polly	Dorothy Ford
Mother	Barbara Brown
Donald	David Stollery
The King	William Farnum
Eloise Larkin and the Princess	Shaye Cogan
Arthur Royal and The Prince	James Alexander
Johnny Conrad and Dancers	
Patrick, The Harp	

Bud Abbott, Shaye Cogan, James Alexander
Center (L. to R.) Buddy Baer, William Farnum
Top: Bud Abbott, Lou Costello, Shaye Cogan,
James Alexander

41

Una Merkel, Thelma Ritter, Susan Hayward, David Wayne
Top: Thelma Ritter, Susan Hayward

(20th CENTURY-FOX)
WITH A SONG IN MY HEART

Producer, Lamar Trotti; Director, Walter Lang; Screenplay by Lamar Trotti; Color by Technicolor; Choreography by Billy Daniel.

CAST

Jane Froman	Susan Hayward
John Burn	Rory Calhoun
Don Ross	David Wayne
Clancy	Thelma Ritter
G. I. Paratrooper	Robert Wagner
Jennifer March	Helen Westcott
Sister Marie	Una Merkel
Tenor	Richard Allan
Guild	Max Showalter
Radio Director	Lyle Talbot
General	Leif Erickson
Texas	Frank Sully

and Eddie Firestone, George Offerman, Beverly Thompson.

Robert Wagner, Susan Hayward

Rory Calhoun, Susan Hayward

(M-G-M)

SKIRTS AHOY

Producer, Joe Pasternak; Director, Sidney Lanfield; Screenplay by Isobel Lennart; Songs by Harry Warren; Lyrics by Ralph Blane; Musical Numbers Created and Staged by Nick Castle; Color by Technicolor.

CAST

Whitney Young	Esther Williams
Mary Kate Yarbrough	Joan Evans
Una Yancy	Vivian Blaine
Lt. Paul Elcott	Barry Sullivan
Dick Hallson	Keefe Brasselle
Billy Eckstine	Himself
Archie O'Conovan	Dean Miller
Lt. Cmdr. Stauton	Margalo Gillmore
The Williams Sisters	The DeMarco Sisters
Lt. Giff	Jeff Donnell
Thatcher Kinston	Thurston Hall
Capt. Graymont	Roy Roberts
Plumber	Emmett Lynn
Doctor	Hayden Rorke
Boy and Girl	Russell and Kathy Tongay

Barry Sullivan, Margalo Gillmore, Vivian B
Top: Esther Williams, Barry Sullivan
Left: Joan Evans, Keefe Brasselle

(WARNER BROS.)

ABOUT FACE

Producer, William Jacobs; Director, Roy Del Ruth; Assistant Director, Mel Dellar; Screenplay by Peter Milne; Based on Play "Brother Rat" by John Monks, Jr. and Fred F. Finklehoffe; Color by Technicolor; Musical Numbers Staged and Directed by LeRoy Prinz; Music by Peter De Rose; Lyrics by Charles Tobias.

CAST

Tony Williams	Gordon MacRae
Boff Roberts	Eddie Bracken
Dave Crouse	Dick Wesson
Betty Long	Virginia Gibson
Alice Wheatley	Phyllis Kirk
Lorna Carter	Aileen Stanley, Jr.
Bender	Joel Grey
Col. Long	Larry Keating
Lt. Jones	Cliff Ferre
Hal Carlton	John Baer

Dick Wesson, Virginia Gibson, Gordon MacRae,
Aileen Stanley, Jr., Eddie Bracken, Phyllis Kirk

Dick Wesson, Virginia Gibson, Aileen Stanley
Gordon MacRae, Eddie Bracken
Center: Gordon MacRae, Dick Wesson

(PARAMOUNT)

ANYTHING CAN HAPPEN

Producer, William Perlberg; Director, George
eaton; Screenplay by George Seaton and
eorge Oppenheimer; From Book by George
nd Helen Papashvily; Music by Victor Young.

CAST

iorgi	Jose Ferrer
elen Watson	Kim Hunter
uri Bey	Kurt Kasznar
nna Godiedze	Eugenie Leontovich
ncle Besso	Oscar Karlweiss
ncle John	Oscar Beregi
ariel Godiedze	Makhail Rasumny
hancho	Nick Dennis
uba Godiedze	Gloria Marlowe
andro	Otto Waldis
avli	Alex Danaroff
adame Greshkin	Natasha Lytess

Eugenie Leontovich, Kim Hunter,
Makhail Rasumny

Kim Hunter, José Ferrer
Top: José Ferrer, Kurt Kasznar

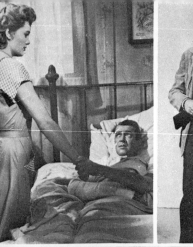

(M-G-M)

CARBINE WILLIAMS

Producer, Armand Deutsch; Director, Rich
Thorpe; Story and Screenplay by Art Co
Music by Conrad Salinger.

CAST

Marsh Williams .... James Stew
Maggie Williams .... Jean Hag
Capt. H. T. Peoples .... Wendell Co
Claude Williams .... Carl Benton R
"Dutch" Kruger .... Paul Stew
Mobley .... Otto Hul
Redwick Karson .... Rhys Willia
Lionell Daniels .... Herbert He
Leon Williams .... James Arn
Sam Markley .... Porter H
David Williams .... Bobby Hy
Feder .... Leif Ericks
District Attorney .... Fay Roo
Andrew White .... Ralph Dum
and Henry Corden, Frank Richards, Howa
Petrie, Stuart Randall, Dan Riss.

Leif Erickson, James Stewart
Top: Jean Hagen, James Stewart; James Stewart

Jean Hagen, James Stewart, Willis Bouch
Wendell Corey

(20th CENTURY-FOX)

THE OUTCASTS
OF POKER FLAT

Producer, Julian Blaustein; Director, Josep
M. Newman; Screenplay by Edmund H. Nort
Based on Story by Bret Harte; Music by Hu
Friedhofer.

CAST

Cal .... Anne Baxt
John Oakhurst .... Dale Robertso
Duchess .... Miriam Hopki
Ryker .... Cameron Mitch
Tom Dakin .... Craig H
Piney .... Barbara Bat
Jake .... William Lyn
Drunk .... Dick Ri
Townsman .... Tom Greenw
Vigilante .... Russ Conw
Bill Akeley .... John Ridgel
Bearded Miner .... Harry T. Shann
George Larabee .... Harry Harvey, S

Barbara Bates, Craig Hill, Anne Baxter,
Miriam Hopkins, Dale Robertson

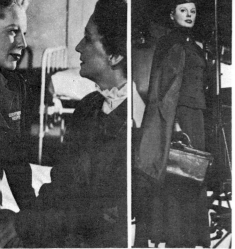

(M-G-M)

THE GIRL IN WHITE

Producer, Armand Deutsch; Director, John Sturges; Screenplay by Irmgard Von Cube and Allen Vincent; Adaptation by Irmgard Von Cube and Philip Stevenson; Based on Book "Bowery to Bellevue" by Emily Dunning Barringer; Music by David Raksin.

CAST

Dr. Emily Dunning	June Allyson
Dr. Ben Barringer	Arthur Kennedy
Dr. Seth Pawling	Gary Merrill
Dr. Marie Yeomans	Mildred Dunnock
Alec	Jesse White
Nurse Jane Doe	Marilyn Erskine
Dr. Barclay	Guy Anderson
Dr. Graham	Gar Moore
Dr. Williams	Don Keefer
Dr. Ellerton	Jonathan Cott
Nurse Bigley	Ann Tyrrell
Matt	James Arness
Commissioner Hawley	Curtis Cooksey

and Carol Brannon, Ann Morrison, Jo Gilbert, Erwin Kalser, Kathryn Card, Joan Valerie, Coleman Francis, A. Cameron Grant, David Fresco.

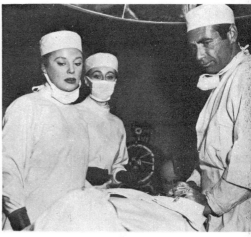

June Allyson, Arthur Kennedy
June Allyson, Mildred Dunnock; June Allyson

June Allyson, Mildred Dunnock, Gary Merrill

(PARAMOUNT)

RED MOUNTAIN

Producer, Hal B. Wallis; Director, William Dieterle; Screenplay by John Meredyth Lucas, George F. Slavin and George W. George; Color by Technicolor.

CAST

Capt. Brett Sherwood	Alan Ladd
Chris	Lizabeth Scott
Lane Waldron	Arthur Kennedy
Quantrell	John Ireland
Skee	Jeff Corey
Dr. Terry	James Bell
Randall	Bert Freed
Benjie	Walter Sande
Dixon	Neville Brand
Morgan	Carleton Young
Miles	Whit Bissell

and Jay Silver Heels, Francis McDonald, Iron Eyes Cody, Herbert Belles, Dan White, Ralph Moody, Crane Whitley.

Alan Ladd, Lizabeth Scott, Arthur Kennedy

THE SAN FRANCISCO STORY

Producer, Howard Welsch; Director, Robert Parrish; Assistant Director, Ben Chapman; Screenplay by D. D. Beauchamp; Based on Novel by Richard Summers; Music by Emil Newman and Paul Dunlap; A Fidelity-Vogue Picture.

CAST

Rick Nelson	Joel McCrea
Adelaide McCall	Yvonne DeCarlo
Andrew Cain	Sidney Blackmer
Shorty	Richard Erdman
Sadie	Florence Bates
Jim Martin	Onslow Stevens
Lessing	John Raven
Alfey	O. Z. Whitehead
Winfield Holbert	Ralph Dumke
Thompson	Robert Foulk
Morton	Lane Chandler
Miner	Trevor Bardette

and John Doucette, Peter Virgo, Frank Hagney, Tor Johnson, Fred Graham.

Sidney Blackmer, Yvonne DeCarlo,
Trevor Bardette, Joe McCrea

THE FIGHTER

Producer, Alex Gottlieb; Director, Herbert Kline; Assistant Director, Emmett Emerson; Screenplay by Aben Kandel and Herbert Kline; Based on "The Mexican" by Jack London.

CAST

Filipe Rivera	Richard Conte
Kathy	Vanessa Brown
Durango	Lee J. Cobb
Paulino	Frank Silvera
Nevis	Roberta Haynes
Roberts	Hugh Sanders
Stella	Claire Carleton
Luis	Martin Garralaga
Maria	Argentina Brunetti
Alvarado	Rudolfo Hoyos, Jr.
Elba	Margaret Padilla
Fierro	Paul Fierro

Richard Conte,
Vanessa Brown

Richard Conte

MARA MARU

Producer, David Weisbart; Director, Gordon Douglas; Assistant Director, William Kissel; Screenplay by N. Richard Nash; Based on Story by Philip Yordan, Sidney Harmon and Hollister Noble; Music by Max Steiner.

CAST

Mason	Errol Flynn
Stella	Ruth Roman
Benedict	Raymond Burr
Steve Ranier	Paul Picerni
Andy Callahan	Richard Webb
Lt. Zuenon	Dan Seymour
Ortega	George Renavent
Manuelo	Robert Cabal
Perol	Henry Marco
Capt. Van Hoten	Nestor Paiva
Felix	Howard Chuman

Ruth Roman, Richard Webb, Errol Flynn

(20th CENTURY-FOX)
DEADLINE - U.S.A.

Producer, Sol C. Siegel; Written and Directed by Richard Brooks; Music by Cyril Mockridge.

CAST

Ed Hutcheson	Humphrey Bogart
Mrs. Garrison	Ethel Barrymore
Nora	Kim Hunter
Frank Allen	Ed Begley
Burrows	Warren Stevens
Thompson	Paul Stewart
Rienzi	Martin Gabel
Schmidt	Joseph De Santis
Kitty Garrison Geary	Joyce MacKenzie
Mrs. Willebrandt	Audrey Christie
Alice Garrison Courtney	Fay Baker
Whitey	Joe Sawyer
Cleary	Jim Backus

and Carleton Young, Selmer Jackson, Fay Roope, Parley Baer, Bette Francine, John Doucette, June Eisner, Richard Monohan, Harry Tyler, Florence Shirley, Kasia Orzazewski, Raymond Greenleaf, Alex Gerry, Irene Vernon, Everett Glass, Tudor Owen, William Forrest, Edward Keane, Clancy Cooper, Tom Powers, Thomas Browne Henry, Ashley Cowan, Howard Negley, Phil Terry, Joe Mell, Luther Crockett, Ann McCrea, Willis Bouchey, Paul Dubov, Harris Brown, Joseph Crehan, Larry Dobkin.

Left: Ed Begley, Joseph DeSantis, Paul Stewart, Humphrey Bogart
Top: Joyce MacKenzie, Fay Baker, Ethel Barrymore

(20th CENTURY-FOX)
BELLES ON THEIR TOES

Producer, Samuel G. Engel; Director, Henry Levin; Screenplay by Phoebe and Henry Ephron; Based on Book by Frank B. Gilbreth, Jr., and Ernestine Gilbreth Carey; Color by Technicolor; Music by Cyril Mockridge.

CAST

Anne Gilbreth	Jeanne Crain
Mrs. Gilbreth	Myrna Loy
Martha	Debra Paget
Dr. Bob Grayson	Jeffrey Hunter
Sam Harper	Edward Arnold
Tom Bracken	Hoagy Carmichael
Ernestine	Barbara Bates
Frank Gilbreth	Robert Arthur
Cousin Leora	Verna Felton
Bob Gilbreth	Carole Nugent
Jane Gilbreth	Tina Thompson
Jack Gilbreth	Teddy Driver
William Gilbreth	Tommy Ivo
Fred Gilbreth	Jimmy Hunt
Dan Gilbreth	Anthony Sydes
Al Lynch	Martin Milner
Martin Dykes	Clay Randolph
Jane (at 22)	June Hedin
Franklyn Dykes	Robert Easton
Emily	Cecil Weston

Left: Jeffrey Hunter, Jeanne Crain
Center: Hoagy Carmichael, Debra Paget, Myrna Loy, Jeanne Crain, Robert Arthur, Barbara Bates

(UNIVERSAL)
NO ROOM FOR THE GROOM

Producer, Ted Richmond; Director, Douglas Sirk; Screenplay by Joseph Hoffman; Based on Story by Darwin L. Teilhet; Music by Frank Skinner.

CAST

Alvah Morrell	Tony Curtis
Lee Kingshead	Piper Laurie
Herman Strouple	Don DeFore
Mama	Spring Byington
Will Stubbins	Jack Kelly
Donovan	Lee Aaker
Elsa	Lillian Bronson
Mr. Taylor	Stephen Chase
Dr. Trotter	Paul McVey

and Lynn Hunter, Fess Parker, Frank Sully, Helen Noyes, Elsie Baker, Fred J. Miller, James Parnell, Lee Turnbull, Janet Clark, Delores Mann, Alice Rickey.

Piper Laurie, Tony Curtis
Center: Piper Laurie, Tony Curtis

Tony Curtis, Piper Laurie

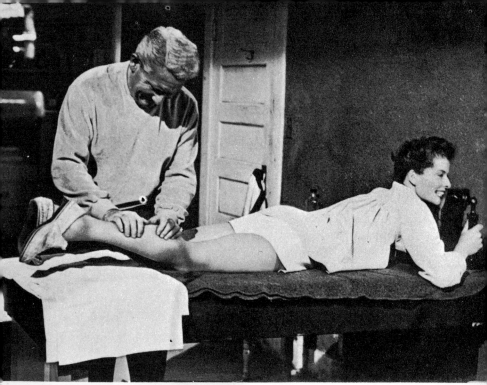

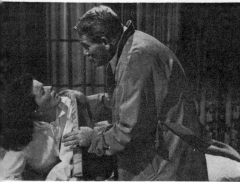

(M-G-M)
PAT AND MIKE

Producer, Lawrence Weingarten; Director, George Cukor; Screenplay by Ruth Gordon and Garson Kanin; Music by David Raksin.

CAST

Mike Conovan	Spencer Tracy
Pat Pemberton	Katharine Hepburn
Davie Hucko	Aldo Ray
Collier Weld	William Ching
Barney Grau	Sammy White
Spec Cauley	George Matthews
Mr. Beminger	Loring Smith
Mrs. Beminger	Phyllis Povah
Hank Tasling	Charles Buchinski
Sam Garsell	Frank Richards
Charles Barry	Jim Backus

and Chuck Connors, Joseph E. Bernard, Owen McGiveney, Lou Lubin, Carl Switzer, William Self, Gussie Moran, Babe Didrikson, Don Budge, Alice Marble, Frank Parker, Betty Hicks, Beverly Hanson, Helen Dettweiler.

William Ching, Katharine Hepburn,
Spencer Tracy
nter & Top: Katharine Hepburn, Spencer Tracy

Aldo Ray, Spencer Tracy, Katharine Hepburn

53

Rock Hudson, Yvonne DeCarlo

(UNIVERSAL)
SCARLET ANGEL

Producer, Leonard Goldstein, Director, Sidney Salkow; Story and Screenplay by Oscar Brodney; Color by Technicolor; Dances by Harold Belfer.

CAST

Roxy McClanahan	Yvonne De Carlo
Frank Truscott	Rock Hudson
Malcolm	Richard Denning
Norton Wade	Whitfield Connor
Linda Caldwell	Bodil Miller
Susan	Amanda Blake
Morgan Caldwell	Henry O'Neill
Eugenie Caldwell	Maude Wallace
Firsby	Dan Riss
Pierre	Henry Brandon
Phineas Calhoun	Tol Avery

Ruth Roman, Glenn Ford, Mary Wickes

(M-G-M)
YOUNG MAN WITH IDEAS

Producers, Gottfried Reinhardt and William H. Wright; Director, Mitchell Leisen; Screenplay by Arthur Sheekman; Music by David Rose.

CAST

Maxwell Webster	Glenn Ford
Julie Webster	Ruth Roman
Dorianne Gray	Denise Darcel
Joyce Laramie	Nina Foch
Caroline Webster	Donna Corcoran
Edmund Jethrow	Ray Collins
Mrs. Gilpin	Mary Wickes
Willis Gilpin	Bobby Diamond
Brick Davis	Sheldon Leonard
Eddie Tasling	Dick Wessel
Tux Cullery	Carl Milletaire
Judge Jennings	Curtis Cooksey
Punchy	Karl Davis
Kyle Thornhill	Fay Roope

and John Call, Nadene Ashdown, Barry Rado, Norman Rado, Wilton Graff, Martha Wentworth.

James Warren, Gloria Swanson, Janine Perreau

(WARNER BROS.)
3 FOR BEDROOM C

Associate Producer, Edward L. Alperson, Jr.; Written and Directed by Milton H. Bren; Assistant Directors, Ben Chapman and Gordon McLean; Based on Novel by Goddard Lieberson; Color in Natural Color; Music by Heinz Roemheld; A Brenco Production.

CAST

Ann Haven	Gloria Swanson
Oli J. Thrumm	James Warren
Johnny Pizer	Fred Clark
Jack Bleck	Hans Conried
Conde Marlow	Steve Brodie
Barbara	Janine Perreau
Fred Johnson	Ernest Anderson
Mrs. Hawthorne	Margaret Dumont

(PARAMOUNT)

THE DENVER AND THE RIO GRANDE

Producer, Nat Holt; Director, Byron Haskin; Story and Screenplay by Frank Gruber; Color by Technicolor.

CAST

Jim Vesser	Edmond O'Brien
McCabe	Sterling Hayden
General Palmer	Dean Jagger
Linda Prescott	Laura Elliott
Johnny Buff	Lyle Bettger
Harkness	J. Carrol Naish
Jane	Zasu Pitts
Sloan	Tom Powers
Haskins	Robert Barrat
Engineer Monyhan	Paul Fix
Bob Nelson	Don Haggerty
Sheriff Masters	James Burke

Laura Elliott, Dean Jagger, Edmond O'Brien

(20th CENTURY-FOX)

KANGAROO

Producer, Robert Bassler; Associate Producer, Robert Snody; Director, Lewis Milestone; Screenplay by Harry Kleiner; Based on Story by Martin Berkeley; Color by Technicolor; Music by Sol Kaplan.

CAST

Dell McGuire	Maureen O'Hara
Richard Connor	Peter Lawford
Michael McGuire	Finlay Currie
Gamble	Richard Boone
Trooper Leonard	Chips Rafferty
Kathleen	Letty Craydon
Matt	Charles Tingwell
Fenner	Ron Whelan
Burke	John Fegan
Pleader	Guy Doleman
Ship's Officer	Reg Collins
Burton	Frank Ransom
Aborgine Stockman	Clyde Combo
Black Tracker	Henry Murdoch

Peter Lawford, Finlay Currie, Maureen O'Hara, Richard Boone

(M-G-M)

GLORY ALLEY

Producer, Nicholas Nayfack; Director, Raoul Walsh; Story and Screenplay by Art Cohn; Choreography by Charles O'Curran.

CAST

Socks Barbarrosa	Ralph Meeker
Angela	Leslie Caron
The Judge	Kurt Kasznar
Peppi Donnato	Gilbert Roland
Gabe Jordan	John McIntire
Shadow Johnson	Louis Armstrong
Jack Teagarden	Himself
Sal Nichols (The Pig)	Dan Seymour
Dr. Robert Ardley	Larry Gates
Jabber	Pat Goldin
Spider	John Indrisano

and Mickey Little, Dick Simmons, Pat Valentino, David McMahon, George Carver.

Ralph Meeker, Leslie Caron

Dale Robertson, Anne Francis, Juanita Moore,
Center: William Marshall, Dale Robertson;
Charles Korvin, Angos Perez, Anne Francis
Top: Anne Francis, Dale Robertson, Charles
Korvin, Adeline deWalt Reynolds

(20th CENTURY-FOX)
LYDIA BAILEY

Producer, Jules Schermer; Director, Jean
Negulesco; Screenplay by Michael Blankfort
and Philip Dunne; Color by Technicolor; Music
by Hugo Friedhofer.

CAST

Albion Hamlin	Dale Robertson
Lydia Bailey	Anne Francis
d'Autremont	Charles Korvin
King Dick	William Marshall
Gen. LeClerc	Luis Van Rooten
Madame d'Autremont	Adeline deWalt Reynolds
Paul	Angos Perez
Soldier	Bob Evans
Pauline Bonaparte	Gladys Holland
Consul	Will Wright
Mirabeau	Roy E. Glenn
Toussaint	Ken Renard
Marie	Juanita Moore

and Carmen de Lavallade, Martin Wilkins, Al-
bert Morin, William Washington, Clancy Cooper,
Muriel Bledsoe, Mildred Boyd, Marjorie Elliott,
Sizette Harbin, Roz Hayes, Dolores Mallory,
Lena Torrence, Frances Williams, Ken Terrell,
Louis Mercier, William Walker, Fred Cavens.

(M-G-M)

SCARAMOUCHE

Producer, Carey Wilson; Director, George Sidney; Screenplay by Ronald Millar and George Froeschel; Based on Novel by Rafael Sabatini; Music by Victor Young; Color by Technicolor.

CAST

Andre Moreau	Stewart Granger
Lenore	Eleanor Parker
Aline De Gavrillac	Janet Leigh
Noel, Marquis De Maynes	Mel Ferrer
Chevalier De Chabrillaine	Henry Wilcoxon
Marie Antoinette	Nina Foch
Philippe De Valmorin	Richard Anderson
Gaston Binet	Robert Coote
Georges De Valmorin	Lewis Stone
Isabelle De Valmorin	Elisabeth Risdon
Michael Vanneau	Howard Freeman
Fabian	Curtis Cooksey
Doutreval	John Dehner
Dr. Dubuque	John Litel
Sergeant	Jonathan Cott

and Dan Foster, Owen McGiveney, Hope Landin, Frank Mitchell, Carol Hughes, Richard Hale.

Lewis Stone, Elisabeth Risdon, Richard Anderson, Stewart Granger
Center: Mel Ferrer, Stewart Granger;
Stewart Granger, Janet Leigh, Mel Ferrer
Top: Stewart Granger, Henry Wilcoxon,
Patrick Conway, Rex Reason, Eleanor Parker

(20th CENTURY-FOX)

DON'T BOTHER TO KNOCK

Producer, Julian Blaustein; Director, Ro▓
▓aker; Screenplay by Daniel Taradash; Base▓
on Novel by Charlotte Armstrong.

CAST

Jed Towers	Richard Widmar▓
Nell	Marilyn Monro▓
Lyn Leslie	Anne Bancrof▓
Bunny	Donna Corcora▓
Rochelle	Jeanne Cagne▓
Mrs. Ruth Jones	Lurene Tuttl▓
Eddie	Elisha Cook, J▓
Peter Jones	Jim Back▓
Mrs. Ballew	Verna Felto▓
Bartender	Willis B. Bouche▓
Mr. Ballew	Don Beddo▓
Girl Photographer	Gloria Blonde▓
Mrs. McMurdock	Grace Hay▓
Pat	Michael Ros▓
Maid	Eda Reis Meri▓
Elevator Operator	Victor Perri▓
Bell Captain	Dick Coga▓
Doorman	Robert Fou▓
Desk Clerk	Olan Sou▓
Toastmaster	Emmett Voga▓

Left: Richard Widmark, Marilyn Monro▓
Top: Anne Bancroft, Marilyn Monroe,
Richard Widmark

(PARAMOUNT)

THE ATOMIC CITY

Producer, Joseph Sistrom; Director, Je▓
Hopper; Screenplay by Sydney Boehm; Mu▓
by Leith Stevens.

CAST

Dr. Frank Addison	Gene Ba▓
Martha Addison	Lydia Cla▓
Tommy Addison	Lee Aa▓
Russ Farley	Michael Mo▓
Ellen Haskell	Nancy Ga▓
Peggy Marston	Bonny Kay E▓
Gregory	Housely Stevenson,
Jablons	Bert Fre▓
Inspector Mann	Milburn Sto▓
Driscoll	Norman Bu▓

and Frank Cady, Leonard Strong, Antho▓
Ward, John Damler, George M. Lynn.

Lydia Clarke, Lee Aaker, Gene Barry
Center: Gene Barry, Lydia Clarke;
58 Housely Stevenson, Jr., Lydia Clarke, Nancy Gates

James Hayter, Richard Todd

James Robertson Justice, Anthony Forwood, Richard Todd

(R K O)
THE STORY OF ROBIN HOOD

Producer, Perce Pearce; Directors, Ken Anna-kin and Alex Bryce; Screenplay by Lawrence E. Watkin; Color by Technicolor; A Walt Disney Production.

CAST

Robert Fitzooth (Robin Hood)	Richard Todd
Maid Marian	Joan Rice
Friar Tuck	James Hayter
Queen Eleanor	Martita Hunt
De Lacy	Peter Finch
Little John	James Robertson Justice
Stutely	Bill Owen
Prince John	Hubert Gregg
Scathelock	Michael Hordern
Allan-a-Dale	Elton Hayes
King Richard I	Patrick Barr

and Reginald Tate, Hal Osmond, Clement Mc-Callin, Louise Hampton, Antony Eustrel, Anthony Forwood.

Richard Todd,
Martita Hunt

Richard Todd

Joan Rice, Richard Todd

Center: (left) Joan Rice, (right) Richard Todd

UNIVERSAL)

FRANCIS GOES
TO WEST POINT

Producer, Leonard Goldstein; Director, A
thur Lubin; Story and Screenplay by Os
Brodney; Additional Dialogue by Dorothy Re
Based on Character "Francis" created by Dav
Stern.

CAST

Peter Stirling	Donald O'Conn
Barbara Atwood	Lori Nels
Cynthia Daniels	Alice Kell
Wilbur Van Allen	William Reyno
William Norton	Palmer L
Col. Daniels	Les Tremay
Corp. Ransom	James B
Chad Chadwick	Otto Hul

Lori Nelson, Donald O'Connor, Palmer Lee
Center: William Reynolds, Donald O'Connor,
Palmer Lee; Donald O'Connor, Francis
Top: Donald O'Connor, Francis

(WARNER BROS.)

THE STORY OF WILL ROGERS

Producer, Robert Arthur; Director, Michael
Curtiz; Assistant Director, Sherry Shourds;
Screenplay by Frank Davis and Stanley Roberts;
Adapted by John C. Moffitt; Based on Saturday
Evening Post Story "Uncle Clem's Boy" by
Will Rogers; Music by Victor Young;
Color by Technicolor.

CAST

Will Rogers	Will Rogers, Jr.
Betty Will Rogers	Jane Wyman
Clem Rogers	Carl Benton Reid
Amy Marshall	Eve Miller
Bert Lynn	James Gleason
Dusty Donovan	Slim Pickens
Wiley Post	Noah Beery, Jr.
Mr. Foster	Mary Wickes
Dave Marshall	Steve Brodie
Eddie Cantor	Himself

Pinky Tomlin, Margaret Field, Virgil S.
Taylor, Richard Kean, Jay Silverheels, William
Forrest, Earl Lee, Brian Daly.

Jane Wyman, Will Rogers, Jr.
Center (L. to R.) Will Rogers, Jr., Jane Wyman;
Will Rogers, Jr., Jane Wyman, Carl Benton Reid
Top (L. to R.) Will Rogers, Jr.; Will Rogers, Jr.,
Noah Beery, Jr.

Lon Chaney, Thomas Mitchell, Henry Morgan, Eve McVeagh, Otto Kruger, Grace Kelly, Garry Cooper

Gary Cooper, Grace Kelly, Katy Jurado

(UNITED ARTISTS)
HIGH NOON

Producer, Stanley Kramer; Director, Fred Zinnemann; Assistant Director, Emmett Emerson; Music by Dimitri Tiomkin; Screenplay by Carl Foreman; Based on Story "The Tin Star" by John W. Cunningham; A Stanley Kramer Production.

CAST

Will Kane	Gary Cooper
Jonas Henderson	Thomas Mitchell
Harvey Pell	Lloyd Bridges
Helen Ramirez	Katy Jurado
Amy Kane	Grace Kelly
Percy Mettrick	Otto Kruger
Martin Howe	Lon Chaney
William Fuller	Henry Morgan
Frank Miller	Ian MacDonald
Mildred Fuller	Eve McVeagh
Cooper	Harry Shannon
Jack Colby	Lee Van Cleef
James Pierce	Bob Wilke
Ben Miller	Sheb Woolley
Sam	Tom London

and Ted Stanhope, Larry Blake, William Phillips, Jeanne Blackford, James Millican, Cliff Clark, Ralph Reed, William Newell, Lucien Prival, Guy Beach, Howland Chamberlin, Morgan Farley, Virginia Christine, Virginia Farmer.

Thomas Mitchell
Center:
62 **Lloyd Bridges,**
Katy Jurado

Gary Cooper, Grace Kelly

Otto Kruger
Center:
Lon Chaney,
Grace Kelly

Gary Cooper in
"High Noon"

(PARAMOUNT)

JUMPING JACKS

Producer, Hal B. Wallis; Director, Norman Taurog; Screenplay by Robert Lees, Fred Rinaldo and Herbert Baker; Additional Dialogue by James Allardice and Richard Weil; Based on Story by Brian Marlow.

CAST

Chick Allen	Dean Martin
Hap Smith	Jerry Lewis
Betty Carter	Mona Freeman
Kelsey	Don DeFore
Sgt. McCluskey	Robert Strauss
Dogface Dolan	Richard Erdman
Gen. Timmons	Ray Teal
Julia Loring	Marcy McGuire
Evans	Danny Arnold
Sam Gilmore	Edwin Max
Earl White	Alex Gerry
Gen. Bond	Charles Evans

Dean Martin, Jerry Lewis, Robert Strau
Center (L. to R.) Dean Martin, Jerry Le
Richard Erdman; Dean Martin, Robert Str
Jerry Lewis, Danny Arnold
Top: Don DeFore, Jerry Lewis, Dean Ma
Robert Strauss

(O)

THE BIG SKY

oducer and Director, Howard Hawks; As-
te Producer, Edward Lasker; Screenplay by
ey Nichols; Based on Novel by A. B.
rie, Jr.; Music by Dimitri Tiomkin; As-
nt Director, William McGarry; A Win-
er Pictures Production.

CAST

ins	Kirk Douglas
e	Dewey Martin
Eye	Elizabeth Threatt
	Arthur Hunnicutt
aine	Buddy Baer
lonnais	Steven Geray
devil	Hank Worden
k	Jim Davis
die	Henri Letondal
quette	Robert Hunter
al	Booth Colman
Masters	Paul Frees
face	Frank de Kova
face	Guy Wilkerson

Dewey Martin, Kirk Douglas, Elizabeth Threatt
Center (L. to R.) Arthur Hunnicutt, Kirk Douglas,
Dewey Martin; Arthur Hunnicutt, Dewey Martin
Top: Kirk Douglas, Dewey Martin   **65**

Kurt Kasznar,
Zsa Zsa Gabor

Marge and Gower
Champion

Red Skelton,
Ann Miller

Top: Kathryn Grayson, Howard Keel, Ann Miller, Red Skelton, Marge and Gower Champio

(M-G-M)

LOVELY TO LOOK AT

Producer, Jack Cummings; Director, Mervyn LeRoy; Screenplay by George Wells and Harry Ruby; Additional Dialogue by Andrew Solt; Based on Musical Comedy "Roberta" from the Novel by Alice Duer Miller; Book and Lyrics by Otto A. Harbach; Music by Jerome Kern; Additional and Revised Lyrics by Dorothy Fields; Choreography by Hermes Pan; Color by Technicolor.

CAST

Stephanie	Kathryn Grayson
Al Marsh	Red Skelton
Tony Naylor	Howard Keel
Clarisse	Marge Champion
Jerry Ralby	Gower Champion
Bubbles Cassidy	Ann Miller
Zsa Zsa	Zsa Zsa Gabor
Max Fogelsby	Kurt Kasznar
Pierre	Marcel Dalio
Diane	Diane Cassidy

Ann Miller, Howard Keel, Kathryn Gray:

(20th CENTURY-FOX)

DIPLOMATIC COURIER

Producer, Casey Robinson; Director, Henry
Hathaway; Screenplay by Casey Robinson and
[Will]iam O'Brien; Based on Novel by Peter Chey-
[n]ey; Music by Sol Kaplan.

CAST

[M]ike Kells .... Tyrone Power
[Jo]an Ross .... Patricia Neal
[Co]l. Cagle .... Stephen McNally
[Ja]nine .... Hildegarde Neff
[Er]nie .... Karl Malden
[Sa]m Carew .... James Millican
[Pl]atov .... Stefan Schnabel
[Gr]nov .... Herbert Berghof
[M]ax Ralli .... Arthur Blake
[St]ewardess .... Helene Stanley
[Ma]n .... Michael Ansara
[Ch]ef De Train .... Sig Arno
[an]d Alfred Linder, Lee Marvin, Peter Coe,
[Ty]ler McVey, Stuart Randall, Dabbs Greer,
[Ca]rleton Young, Charles La Torre, Russ Con-
[w]ay, Tom Powers, Monique Chantal, Lumsden
[H]are.

**Right: Stefan Schnabel, Tyrone Power,
Hildegarde Neff**
Top: Tyrone Power, Patricia Neal

(WARNER BROS.)

SHE'S WORKING HER WAY
THROUGH COLLEGE

[P]roducer, William Jacobs; Director, Bruce
[Hu]mberstone; Assistant Director, Don Page;
[Scr]eenplay by Peter Milne; Adapted from "The
[Ma]le Animal" by James Thurber and Elliott
[Nu]gent; Color by Technicolor; Lyrics by Sammy
[Ca]hn; Music by Vernon Duke; Musical Num-
[ber]s Staged and Directed by LeRoy Prinz.

CAST

[An]gela Gardner .... Virginia Mayo
[Jo]hn Palmer .... Ronald Reagan
[Don] Weston .... Gene Nelson
[Shep] Slade .... Don DeFore
[Hel]en Palmer .... Phyllis Thaxter
[...] Williams .... Patrice Wymore
[Fre]d Copeland .... Roland Winters
[Do]n Rogers .... Raymond Greenleaf
["Iv]y" Gordon .... Norman Bartold
[Spe]cialty .... The Blackburn Twins
[Isa]belle .... Amanda Randolph
[P]rofessor .... George Meader
[Secr]etary .... Eve Miller

Patrice Wymore   **Virginia Mayo**
**Center (L. to R.) Gene Nelson, Virginia Mayo;
Ronald Reagan, Phyllis Thaxter, Don DeFore**

67

Hugh Marlowe, David Wayne, Jean Peters

(20th CENTURY-FOX)

WAIT TILL THE SUN SHINES NELLIE

Producer, George Jessel; Director, Henr
King; Screenplay by Allan Scott; Adaptation b
Allan Scott and Maxwell Shane; Based on Nove
by Ferdinand Reyher; Color by Technicolor
Music by Alfred Newman.

CAST

Nellie	Jean Peter
Ben Halper	David Wayn
Ed Jordan	Hugh Marlow
Lloyd Slocum	Albert Dekke
Eadie Jorda	Helene Stanle
Benny Halper, Jr. (20)	Tommy Morto
Bessie Jordan	Joyce MacKenzi
George Oliphant	Alan Hale, J
Kava	Richard Karla
Adeline	Merry Ande
Austin	Jim Malone
McCauley	Warren Stever
Mr. Burdge	Charles Wat
Sam Eichenbogen	David Wol
Doc Thomas	Dan Whi

and Erik Nielsen, Jerrylyn Flannery, Noree
Corcoran, William Walker, James Griffith, Ke
mit Echols, Eugene Mazola, Tony Barr, Maud
Prickett, Mary Hain.

Janice Rule, Gig Young, Keenan Wynn

(M-G-M)

HOLIDAY FOR SINNERS

Producer, John Houseman; Director, Gera
Mayer; Screenplay by A. I. Bezzerides; Bas
on Novel by Hamilton Basso.

CAST

Jason Kent	Gig You
Joe Piavi	Keenan Wy
Susan Corvier	Janice Ru
Danny Farber	William Campb
Father Victor	Richard Anders
Dr. Konndorff	Michael Chekh
Nick Muto	Sandro Gig
Mrs. Corvier	Edith Barr
Louie	Porter H
Mike Hennighan	Ralph Dum
The Wiry Man	Frank DeKo
Man With Cigar	Will Wri
Dr. Surtees	Jack Ra

Patricia Collinge, Van Johnson, Patricia Neal

(M-G-M)

WASHINGTON STORY

Producer, Dore Schary; Written and Direc
by Robert Pirosh; Music by Conrad Salinge

CAST

Joseph T. Gresham	Van John
Alice Kingsly	Patricia N
Charles W. Birch	Louis Calh
Philip Emery	Sidney Blackr
Gilbert Nunnally	Philip O
Miss Galbreth	Patricia Colli
Speaker	Moroni O
Miss Dee	Elizabeth Patter
Peter Kralik	Reinhold Schur
Caswell	Fay Ro
Bill Holmby	Dan
Mrs. Varick	Joan Ba
John Sheldon	Raymond Green
Mrs. Birch	Katharine Wa
Rodney Delwick	Gregory Mars
Secretary	Perry Shee
Mr. Watkins, Mailman	Jimmie

Charlton Heston, Betty Hutton in
"The Greatest Show On Earth"

Cornel Wilde, James Stewart, Betty Hutton, Charlton Heston, Gloria Grahame
Center (L. to R.): Lyle Bettger, Gloria Grahame; Emmett Kelly, James Stewart
Top: Cornel Wilde, Betty Hutton, Charlton Heston

(PARAMOUNT)

THE GREATEST SHOW ON EARTH

Producer-Director, Cecil B. DeMille; Associate Producer, Henry Wilcoxon; Assistant Director, Edward Salven; Screenplay by Fredric M. Frank, Barre Lyndon and Theodore St. John; Choreography by Richard Barstow; Circus Musical and Dance Numbers Staged by John Murray Anderson; Music by Victor Young; Color by Technicolor; Produced with the cooperation of Ringling Bros.-Barnum & Bailey Circus.

CAST

Holly	Betty Hutton
Sebastian	Cornel Wilde
Brad	Charlton Heston
Phyllis	Dorothy Lamour
Angel	Gloria Grahame
Buttons (A Clown)	James Stewart
Detective	Henry Wilcoxon
Klaus	Lyle Bettger
Henderson	Lawrence Tierney
Harry	John Kellogg
Ass't Manager	John Ridgely
Circus Doctor	Frank Wilcox
Ringmaster	Bob Carson
Button's Mother	Lillian Albertson
Birdie	Julia Faye
Themselves:	Emmett Kelly, Cucciola, Antoinette Concello, John Ringling North

orothy Lamour   Cornel Wilde, Betty Hutton   Cornel Wilde

Center: (left) Betty Hutton, (right) James Stewart
Top: Gloria Grahame, Emmett Kelly, Betty Hutton, Cornel Wilde, Dorothy Lamour, Lyle Bettger

71

(20th CENTURY-FOX)
DREAMBOAT

Producer, Sol C. Siegel; Director, Claude Binyon; Screenplay by Claude Binyon; Based on Story by John D. Weaver; Music, Cyril Mockridge.

CAST

Thornton Sayre	Clifton Webb
Gloria	Ginger Rogers
Carol Sayre	Anne Francis
Bill Ainslee	Jeffrey Hunter
Dr. Coffey	Elsa Lanchester
Sam Levitt	Fred Clark
Harrington	Paul Harvey
Timothy Stone	Ray Collins
Mimi	Helene Stanley
Judge Bowles	Richard Garrick
Commandant	George Barrow
Desk Clerk	Jay Adler
Lavinia	Marietta Canty
Mrs. Gunther	Laura Brook
Used Car Salesman	Emory Parnel

and Helen Hatch, Harry Cheshire, Everett Glass, Paul Maxey, Sander Szabo, Leo Clary, Lee Turnbull, Helen Brown, Al Herman, Howard Banks, Jack Mather, Matt Mattox, Frank Radcliffe, Bob Easton, Marjorie Halliday.

Left: Ginger Rogers, Sander Szabo, Clifton W
Top: Ginger Rogers, Anne Francis, Jeffrey H

(UNITED ARTISTS)
ACTORS AND SIN

Produced, Directed and Screenplay by Ben Hecht; Based on two Short Stories by Ben Hecht; A Sid Kuller Production; Music by George Antheil.

CAST
ACTOR'S BLOOD

Maurice Tillayou	Edward G. Robinson
Marcia Tillayou	Marsha Hunt
Alfred O'Shea	Dan O'Herlihy
Otto Lachsley	Rudolph Anders
Tommy	Alice Key
Clyde Veering	Rick Roman

and Peter Brocco, Elizabeth Root, Joe Mell, Irene Martin, Herb Bernard, Bob Carson.

WOMAN OF SIN

Orlando Higgens	Eddie Albert
J. B. Cobb	Alan Reed
Miss Flannigan	Tracey Roberts
Mr. Blue	Paul Guilfoyle
Mr. Devlin	Doug Evans
Mrs. Egelhofer	Jody Gilbert
Daisy Marcher	Jenny Hecht

and George Baxter, George Keymas, Toni Carroll, John Crawford, Kathleen Mulqueen, Alan Mendez, Sam Rosen.

Left: Jody Gilbert, Eddie Albert, Jenny H
Center: Dan O'Herlihy, Marsha Hunt,
Edward G. Robinson

(20th CENTURY-FOX)
WE'RE NOT MARRIED

Producer, Nunnally Johnson; Director, Edmund Goulding; Screenplay by Nunnally Johnson; Adapted by Dwight Taylor; From a Story by Gina Kaus and Jay Dratler; Music, Cyril Mockridge.

CAST

Ramona	Ginger Rogers
Steve Gladwyn	Fred Allen
Justice of The Peace	Victor Moore
Annabel Norris	Marilyn Monroe
Jeff Norris	David Wayne
Katie Woodruff	Eve Arden
Hector Woodruff	Paul Douglas
Willie Fisher	Eddie Bracken
Patsy Fisher	Mitzi Gaynor
Freddie Melrose	Louis Calhern
Eve Melrose	Zsa Zsa Gabor
Duffy	James Gleason
Attorney Stone	Paul Stewart
Mrs. Bush	Jane Darwell
Detective Magnus	Alan Bridge
Radio Announcer	Harry Goler
Governor Bush	Victor Sutherland
Attorney General	Tom Powers

and Maurice Cass, Maude Wallace, Margie Liszt, Richard Buckley, Ralph Dumke, Lee Marvin, Marjorie Weaver, O. Z. Whitehead, Harry Harvey, Selmer Jackson.

er Jackson, Mitzi Gaynor, Harry Harvey

Center: Louis Calhern, Zsa Zsa Gabor
Top: Jane Darwell, Ginger Rogers, Victor Moore, Fred Allen

(PARAMOUNT)

SON OF PALEFACE

Producer, Robert L. Welch; Director, Frank
Tashlin; Screenplay by Frank Tashlin, Robert
L. Welch and Joseph Quillan; Color by Techni-
color; Dances Staged by Josephine Earl; Music
by Lyn Murray, Jay Livingston and Ray Evans,
Jack Brooks, Jack Hope and Lyle Moraine.

CAST

Junior	Bob Hope
Mike	Jane Russell
Roy Rogers	Himself
Kirk	Bill Williams
Doc Lovejoy	Lloyd Corrigan
Ebenezer Hawkins	Paul E. Burns
Sheriff McIntyre	Douglas Dumbrille
Stoner	Harry Von Zell
Indian Chief	Iron Eyes Cody
Blacksmith	Wee Willie Davis
Charley	Charley Cooley

Bob Hope
Right: Jane Russell, Bob Hope, Bill Williams

Roy Rogers, Jane Russell, Bob Hope

Bob Hope, Jane Russell

BIG JIM McLAIN

Producer, Robert Fellows; Director, Edward Ludwig; Assistant Director, Andrew McLaglen; Written by James Edward Grant, Richard English and Eric Taylor; A Wayne-Fellows Production.

CAST

Big Jim McLain	John Wayne
Nancy Vallon	Nancy Olson
Mal Baxter	James Arness
Sturak	Alan Napier
Madge	Veda Ann Borg
Dr. Gelster	Gayne Whitman
Poke	Hal Baylor
Edwin White	Robert Keys
Robert Henried	Hans Conried
Lt. Comdr. Clint Grey	John Hubbard
Mrs. Lexiter	Sara Padden
Mrs. Nomaka	Mme. Soo Yong

and Dan Liu, Paul Hurst, Vernon McQueen.

Zinco Simunovich, Jim Arness
: John Wayne, Paul Hurst, Sarah Padden,
Jim Arness
Right: John Wayne, Veda Ann Borg

John Wayne, Nancy Olson

(UNIVERSAL)

HAS ANYBODY SEEN MY GAL

Producer, Ted Richmond; Director, Douglas Sirk; Screenplay by Joseph Hoffman; Based on Story by Eleanor H. Porter; Color by Technicolor; Dance Director, Harold Belfer.

CAST

Samuel Fulton	Charles Coburn
Millicent Blaisdell	Piper Laurie
Roberta Blaisdell	Gigi Perreau
Dan Stebbins	Rock Hudson
Harriet Blaisdell	Lynn Bari
Charles Blaisdell	Larry Gates
Howard Blaisdell	William Reynolds
Edward Norton	Frank Ferguson
Carl Pennock	Skip Homeier
Clarissa Pennock	Natalie Schafer
Judge Wilkins	Paul Harvey
Quinn	Forrest Lewis

Piper Laurie, Charles Coburn, Rock Hue

(COLUMBIA)

CALIFORNIA CONQUEST

Producer, Sam Katzman; Director, Lew Landers; Screenplay by Robert E. Kent; Color by Technicolor; Music by Mischa Bakaleinikoff.

CAST

Don Arturo Bordega	Cornel Wilde
Julia Lawrence	Teresa Wright
Jose Martinez	Alfonso Bedoya
Helena de Gagarine	Lisa Ferraday
Ernesto Brios	Eugene Iglesias
Fredo Brios	John Dehner
Alexander Rotcheff	Ivan Lebedeff
Don Bernardo Mirana	Tito Renaldo
Fray Lindos	Renzo Cesana
Ignacio	Baynes Barron

and Rico Alaniz, William P. Wilkerson, Edward Colmans, Alex Montoya, Hank Patterson, George Eldredge.

Cornel Wilde, Teresa Wright

(UNIVERSAL)

THE WORLD IN HIS ARMS

Producer, Aaron Rosenberg; Director, Raoul Walsh; Screenplay by Borden Chase; Additional Dialogue by Horace McCoy; Based on Novel by Rex Beach; Color by Technicolor; Dances by Harold Belfer; Music by Frank Skinner.

CAST

Jonathan Clark	Gregory Peck
Countess Marina Selanova	Ann Blyth
Portugee	Anthony Quinn
Deacon Greathouse	John McIntire
Mamie	Andrea King
Prince Semvon	Carl Esmond
Anna	Eugenie Leontovich
Gen. Ivan Vorashilov	Sig Ruman
Eustace	Hans Conried
William Cleggett	Bryan Forbes
Eben Cleggett	Rhys Williams
Ogeechuk	Bill Radovich
Paul Shushaldin	Gregory Gay
Peter	Henry Kulky

Carl Esmond, Ann Blyth, Gregory Pec

Robert Shackleton, Ray Bolger

Ray Bolger, Robert Shackleton, Allyn McLerie, Mary Germaine

(WARNER BROS.)

WHERE'S CHARLEY?

Director, David Butler; Assistant Director, Phil Quinn; Screenplay by John Monks, Jr.; Based on Musical Play of the same name; Music and Lyrics by Frank Loesser; Dance and Production Numbers Staged by Michael Kidd; Color by Technicolor.

CAST

Charley Wykeham	Ray Bolger
Amy Spettigue	Allyn McLerie
Jack Chesney	Robert Shackleton
Stephen Spettigue	Horace Cooper
Dona Lucia	Margaretta Scott
Sir Francis Chesney	Howard Marion Crawford
Kitty Verdun	Mary Germaine
Brassett	Henry Hewitt
Wilkinson	H. G. Stoker
Photographer	Martin Miller

Allyn McLerie, Ray Bolger, Mary Germaine

Ray Bolger

Ray Bolger

Ray Bolger

Cameron Mitchell, Michael Rennie

Below: Robert Newton, Michael Rennie

Michael Rennie, Charles Keane, Edmund G
Norma Varden, Elsa Lanchester
Below: Sylvia Sidney, Michael Rennie,
Robert Newton

(20th CENTURY-FOX)

LES MISERABLES

Producer, Fred Kohlmar; Director, Lewis
Milestone; Screenplay by Richard Murphy;
Based on Novel by Victor Hugo; Music, Alex
North.

CAST

Jean Valjean	Michael Rennie
Cosette	Debra Paget
Javert	Robert Newton
Bishop	Edmund Gwenn
Fantine	Sylvia Sidney
Marius	Cameron Mitchell
Madame Magloire	Elsa Lanchester
Robert	James Robertson Justice
Genflou	Joseph Wiseman
Brevet	Rhys Williams
Madame Bonnet	Florence Bates
Cicely	Merry Anders
Bonnet	John Rogers
Corporal	Charles Keane
Bosun	John Dierkes

and John Costello, Norma Varden, William Cottrell, Queenie Leonard, Bobby Hyatt, Sanders
Clark.

Cameron Mitchell, Michael Rennie

Eddie Albert, Jennifer Jones

Laurence Olivier, Jennifer Jones

Below: Laurence Olivier

Below: Jennifer Jones, Laurence Olivier

(PARAMOUNT)

CARRIE

Producer-Director, William Wyler; Screenplay y Ruth and Augustus Goetz; Based on Novel Sister Carrie."

CAST

eorge Hurstwood	Laurence Olivier
arrie Meeber	Jennifer Jones
lie Hurstwood	Miriam Hopkins
harles Drouet	Eddie Albert
r. Fitzgerald	Basil Ruysdael
lan	Ray Teal
awson	Barry Kelley
rs. Oransky	Sara Berner
eorge Hurstwood, Jr.	William Regnolds
ssica Hurstwood	Mary Murphy
'Brien	Harry Hayden
arrie's Father	Walter Baldwin
arrie's Mother	Dorothy Adams
innie	Jacqueline de Wit

d Harlan Briggs, Melinda Plowman, Donald rr, Lester Sharpe, Don Beddoe, John Alvin.

Laurence Olivier, Jennifer Jones

Joan Crawford, Jack Palance

Gloria Grahame, Touch Connors

Joan Crawford
Jack Palance

Joan Crawford
Jack Palance

Jack Palance

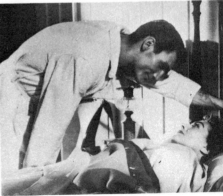

Jack Palance, Joan Crawford, Bruce Bennett

Jack Palance, Joan Crawford

(RKO)

SUDDEN FEAR

Producer, Joseph Kaufman; Director, David Miller; Assistant Director, Ivan Volkman; Screenplay by Lenore Coffee and Robert Smith; Based on Story by Edna Sherry; Music by Elmer Bernstein.

CAST

Myra Hudson	Joan Crawford
Lester Blaine	Jack Palance
Irene Neves	Gloria Grahame
Steve Kearney	Bruce Bennett
Ann Taylor	Virginia Huston
Junior Kearney	Touch Connors

Joan Crawford

(20th CENTURY-FOX)
WHAT PRICE GLORY

Producer, Sol C. Siegel; Director, John Ford; Screenplay by Phoebe and Henry Ephron; Based on Play by Maxwell Anderson and Laurence Stallings; Songs by Jay Livingston and Ray Evans; Color by Technicolor; Dances by Billy Daniel.

CAST

Capt. Flagg	James Cagney
Charmaine	Corinne Calvet
Sgt. Quirt	Dan Dailey
Cpl. Kiper	William Demarest
Lt. Aldrich	Craig Hill
Lewisohn	Robert Wagner
Nicole	Marisa Pavan
Lt. Moore	Casey Adams
Gen. Cokely	James Gleason
Lipinsky	Wally Vernon
Cognac Pete	Henri Letondal
Lt. Schmidt	Fred Libby
Mulcahy	Ray Hyke
Gowdy	Paul Fix
Moran	Henry Morgan

and James Lilburn, Dan Borzage, Bill Henry, Henry Kulky, Jack Pennick, Stanley Johnson, Ann Codee, Tom Tyler, Olga Andre, Barry Norton, Luis Alberni, Torben Meyer, Alfred Zeisler, George Bruggeman, Scott Forbes, Sean McClory, Charles Fitzsimmons, Louis Mercier, Mickey Simpson.

Robert Wagner, Dan Dailey, Marisa Pavan
Right: William Demarest, James Cagney
Center: Corinne Calvet, Dan Dailey
Top: James Cagney, Henri Letondal,
Casey Adams, Dan Dailey

(M-G-M)
YOU FOR ME

Producer, Henry Berman; Director, Don Weis; Assistant Director, Joel Freeman; Story and Screenplay by William Roberts.

CAST

Tony Brown	Peter Lawford
Katie McDermad	Jane Greer
Dr. Jeff Chadwick	Gig Young
Lucille Brown	Paula Corday
Oliver Wherry	Howard Wendell
Hugo McDermad	Otto Hulett
Edna McDermad	Barbara Brown
Ann Elcott	Barbara Ruick
Nurse Vogel	Kathryn Card
Rollie Cobb	Tommy Farrell
Frank Elcott	Paul Smith
Flora Adams	Helen Winston
Girl in Club Car	Elaine Stewart
Nurse	Perry Sheehan

Peter Lawford, Jane Greer, Tommy Farrell
Paul Smith

(UNIVERSAL)

LOST IN ALASKA

Producer, Howard Christie; Director, Jean Yarbrough; Screenplay by Martin Ragaway and Leonard Stern; Story by Elwood Ullman; Musical Numbers Staged by Harold Belfer.

CAST

Tom Watson	Bud Abbott
George Bell	Lou Costello
Rosette	Mitzi Green
Nugget Joe McDermott	Tom Ewell
Jake Stillman	Bruce Cabot
Mrs. McGillicuddy	Minerva Urecal
Sherman	Emory Parnell
Willie	Michael Ross

Lou Costello, Bud Abbott
Left Center: Tom Ewell, Bud Abbott, Lou Costel
Top: Lou Costello, Mitzi Green

(M-G-M)

FEARLESS FAGAN

Producer, Edwin H. Knopf; Associate Producer, Sidney Franklin, Jr.; Director, Stanley Donen; Screenplay by Charles Lederer; Adaptation by Frederick Hazlitt Brennan; Based on Story by Sidney Franklin, Jr.; and Eldon W. Griffiths.

CAST

Abby Ames	Janet Leigh
Pvt. Floyd Hilston	Carleton Carpenter
Sgt. Kellwin	Keenan Wynn
Capt. Daniels	Richard Anderson
Mrs. Ardley	Ellen Corby
Nurse	Barbara Ruick
Mr. Ardley	John Call
Owen Gillman	Robert Burton
Col. Horne	Wilton Graff
Emil Tauchnitz	Parley Baer
Cpl. Geft	Jonathan Cott

Carleton Carpenter, Janet Leigh

John Wayne, Maureen O'Hara
Top: Barry Fitzgerald, John Wayne,
Maureen O'Hara

Jack McGowran, Victor McLaglen, Ward Bond,
Barry Fitzgerald, John Wayne, James Lilburn

(REPUBLIC)

THE QUIET MAN

Producer, Merian C. Cooper; Director, John Ford; Screenplay by Frank S. Nugent; Based on Story by Maurice Walsh; Music by Victor Young; Color by Technicolor; An Argosy Production.

CAST

Sean Thornton	John Wayne
Mary Kate Danaher	Maureen O'Hara
Michaeleen Flynn	Barry Fitzgerald
Father Lonergan	Ward Bond
"Red" Will Danaher	Victor McLaglen
Mrs. Tillane	Mildred Natwick
Tobin	Francis Ford
Mrs. Playfair	Eileen Crowe
The Woman	May Craig
Rev. Playfair	Arthur Shields
Forbes	Charles fitzSimons
Father Paul	James Lilburn
Owen Glynn	Sean McGlory
Feeney	Jack McGowran
Guard	Joseph O'Dea
Engine Driver	Eric Gorman
Fireman	Kevin Lawless
Porter	Paddy O'Donnell
Station Master	Web Overlander

Maureen O'Hara, John Wayne; Right: Victor McLaglen, John Wayne; Top: Victor McLaglen, Mildred Natwick, Barry Fitzgerald

(M-G-M)
THE MERRY WIDOW

Producer, Joe Pasternak; Director, Curtis Bernhardt; Screenplay by Sonya Levien and William Ludwig; Based on Operetta by Franz Lehar and Victor Leon and Leo Stein; Music by Franz Lehar; Lyrics by Paul Francis Webster; Musical Numbers Created and Staged by Jack Cole; Color by Technicolor.

CAST

Crystal Radek	Lana Turner
Count Danilo	Fernando Lamas
Kitty Riley	Una Merkel
Baron Popoff	Richard Haydn
King of Marshovia	Thomas Gomez
Marshovian Ambassador	John Abbott
Police Sergeant	Marcel Dalio
Nitki	King Donovan
Marquis De Crillon	Robert Coote
Gypsy Girl	Sujata
Marcella	Lisa Ferraday
Kunjany	Shepard Menken
Major Domo	Ludwig Stossel

Lana Turner

Una Merkel, Lana Turner, Fernando Lamas
Richard Haydn
Top: Lana Turner, Una Merkel

(UNITED ARTISTS)

ISLAND OF DESIRE

Producer, David E. Rose; Director, Stuart Heisler; Assistant Director, George Fowler; Screenplay by Stephanie Nordli; Based on Novel "Saturday Island" by Hugh Brooke; Color by Technicolor; A Coronado Production.

CAST

Elizabeth Smythe	Linda Darnell
Michael J. "Chicken" Dugan	Tab Hunter
William Peck	Donald Gray
Grimshaw	John Laurie
Tukua	Sheila Chong
Dr. Snyder	Russell Waters
Ollie	Hilda Fenemore
Jane	Brenda Hogan
Mike	Diana Decker
Maggie	Peggy Hassard
Eddie	Michael Newell

Linda Darnell, Tab Hunter
Donald Gray, Tab Hunter, Linda Darnell

Tab Hunter, Donald Gray, Linda Darnell

(UNIVERSAL)
UNTAMED FRONTIER

Producer, Leonard Goldstein; Director, Hugo Fregonese; Screenplay by Gerald Drayson Adams and John and Gwen Bagni; Story by Houston Branch and Eugenia Night; Additional Dialogue by Polly James; Music by Hans J. Salter; Color by Technicolor.

CAST

Kirk Denbow	Joseph Cotten
Jane Stevens	Shelley Winters
Glenn Denbow	Scott Brady
Lottie	Suzan Ball
Matt Denbow	Minor Watson
Camilla Denbow	Katherine Emery
Bandera	Antonio Moreno
Clayton Vance	Douglas Spencer
Max Wickersham	John Alexander
Charlie Fentress	Richard Garland
Dave Chittun	Lee Van Cleef
Ezra	Robert Anderson
Clem	Fess Parker

Scott Brady, Shelley Winters

(20th CENTURY-FOX)
LURE OF THE WILDERNESS

Producer, Robert L. Jacks; Associate Producer, Robert D. Webb; Director, Jean Negulesco; Screenplay by Louis Lantz; Based on a Story by Vereen Bell; Color by Technicolor; Music, Franz Waxman.

CAST

Laurie Harper	Jean Peters
Ben Tyler	Jeffrey Hunter
Noreen	Constance Smith
Jim Harper	Walter Brennan
Zack Taylor	Tom Tully
Pat McGowan	Harry Shannon
Sheriff Brink	Will Wright
Dave Longden	Jack Elam
Ned Tyler	Harry Carter
Harry Longden	Pat Hogan
Shep Rigby	Al Thompson
Will Stone	Robert Adler

and Sherman Sanders, Mary Parker, Robert Karnes, George Spaulding, Walter Taylor, Ted Jordan.

Jeffrey Hunter, Jean Peters

(R K O)
ONE MINUTE TO ZERO

Producer, Edmund Grainger; Director, Tay Garnett; Screenplay by Milton Krims and William Wister Haines; Music by Victor Young.

CAST

Col. Steve Janowski	Robert Mitchum
Linda Day	Ann Blyth
Col. John Parker	William Talman
Sgt. Baker	Charles McGraw
Mary Parker	Margaret Sheridan
Capt. Ralston	Richard Egan
Gustav Engstrand	Eduard Franz
Major Davis	Robert Osterloh
Major Carter	Robert Gist

Eddie Firestone, Tom Irish, William Talman
Robert Mitchum

(UNIVERSAL)

BONZO GOES TO COLLEGE

Producer, Ted Richmond; Assistant Director, Jesse Hibbs; Director, Frederick de Cordova; screenplay by Leo Lieberman and Jack Henley; story by Leo Lieberman; Based on Characters created by Raphael David Blau and Ted Berkman.

CAST

Marion Drew	Maureen O'Sullivan
Pop Drew	Edmund Gwenn
Malcolm Drew	Charles Drake
Betsy Drew	Gigi Perreau
Clarence B. Gateson	Gene Lockhart
Nancy	Irene Ryan
Ronald Calkins	Guy Williams
Wilbur Crane	John Miljan
Jack	David Janssen
Lefty Edwards	Jerry Paris
Dick	Frank Nelson
and Bonzo	

Edmund Gwenn, Bonzo, Gene Lockhart, Gigi Perreau

UNIVERSAL)

SON OF ALI BABA

Producer, Leonard Goldstein; Associate Producer, Ross Hunter; Director, Kurt Neumann; story and Screenplay by Gerald Drayson Adams; color by Technicolor; Musical Numbers Staged by Harold Belfer.

CAST

Kashma Baba	Tony Curtis
Kiki	Piper Laurie
Tala	Susan Cabot
Mustafa	William Reynolds
Hussein	Hugh O'Brian
Caliph	Victor Jory
Ali Baba	Morris Ankrum
Gareeb	Philip Van Zandt
Abu	Leon Belasco
Farouk	Palmer Lee
Neda	Barbara Knudson
Valu	Alice Kelley
Capt. Youssef	Gerald Mohr
Raza	Milada Mladova
Princess Karma	Katherine Warren
Commandant	Robert Barratt

Piper Laurie, Tony Curtis

(PARAMOUNT)

CARIBBEAN

Producers, William Pine and William Thomas; Director, Edward Ludwig; Screenplay by Frank L. Moss and Edward Ludwig; Based on novel by Ellery H. Clark; Color by Technicolor; Music by Lucien Cailliet.

CAST

Dick Lindsay	John Payne
Christine	Arlene Dahl
Barclay	Cedric Hardwicke
Allister	Francis S. Sullivan
Aveley	Willard Parker
Rexford	Dennis Hoey
Quashy	Clarence Muse
Robert McAllister	William Pullen
Evans	Walter Reed
Townsend	Ramsey Hill
Stewart	John Hart
Zaku	Woody Strode

John Payne, Arlene Dahl

Susan Hayward, Gregory Peck
Right: Ava Gardner, Gregory Peck
Top Right: Gregory Peck, Susan Hayward

(20th CENTURY-FOX)

THE SNOWS OF KILIMANJARO

Producer, Darryl F. Zanuck; Director, Henry King; Screenplay by Casey Robinson; Color by Technicolor; Music, Bernard Herrmann; Choreography, Antonio Triana.

CAST

Harry	Gregory Peck
Helen	Susan Hayward
Cynthia	Ava Gardner
Countess Liz	Hildegarde Neff
Uncle Bill	Leo G. Carroll
Johnson	Torin Thatcher
Beatrice	Ava Norring
Connie	Helene Stanley
Emile	Marcel Dalio
Guitarist	Vincent Gomez
Spanish Dancer	Richard Allan
Dr. Simmons	Leonard Carey
Witch Doctor	Paul Thompson
Molo	Emmett Smith
Marquis	Ivan Lebedeff

and Victor Wood, Bert Freed, Agnes Laury, Monique Chantal, Janine Grandel, John Dodsworth, Charles Bates, Lisa Ferraday, Maya Van Horn.

Torin Thatcher, Ava Gardner, Gregory Peck

Hildegarde Neff, Ava Noring, Leo G. Carro
Center: Gregory Peck, Hildegarde Neff

90

(20th CENTURY-FOX)

O. HENRY'S FULL HOUSE

THE COP AND THE ANTHEM

Producer, Andre Hakim; Director, Henry Koster; Screenplay by Lamar Trotti; Music, Alfred Newman.

CAST

Soapy	Charles Laughton
Streetwalker	Marilyn Monroe
Horace	David Wayne
Manager	Thomas Browne Henry
Headwaiter	Richard Karlan
Waiter	Erno Verebes
Owner	Nico Lek
Judge	William Vedder
Bystander	Billy Wayne

THE CLARION CALL

Producer, Andre Hakim; Director, Henry Hathaway; Screenplay by Richard Breen; Music, Alfred Newman; Assistant Director, David Silver.

CAST

Barney Woods	Dale Robertson
Johnny Kernan	Richard Widmark
Hazel	Joyce MacKenzie
Chief of Detectives	Richard Rober
Manager	Will Wright
Bascom	House Peters, Sr.
O. Henry	Tyler McVey
Guard	Phil Tully
Waiter	Frank Cusack
Detective	Stuart Randall
Bartender	Abe Dinovitch

Lee Aaker, Oscar Levant, Fred Allen

Jeanne Crain, Farley Granger

Top: Dale Robertson, Richard Widmark

THE RANSOM OF RED CHIEF

Producer, Andre Hakim; Director, Howard Hawks; Assistant Director, Paul Helmick; Narration by John Steinbeck; Music, Alfred Newman.

CAST

Sam	Fred Allen
Bill	Oscar Levant
J. B.	Lee Aaker
Mr. Dorset	Irving Bacon
Mrs. Dorset	Kathleen Freeman
Storekeeper	Alfred Mizner

THE LAST LEAF

Producer, Andre Hakim; Director, Jean Negulesco; Screenplay by Ivan Goff and Ben Roberts; Assistant Director, Jasper Blystone; Music, Alfred Newman.

CAST

Joanna	Anne Baxter
Susan	Jean Peters
Behrman	Gregory Ratoff
Doctor	Richard Garrick
Radolf	Steven Geray
Dandy	Hal. J. Smith
Mrs. O'Brien	Martha Wentworth
Sheldon Sidney	Bert Hicks
Neighbor	Ruth Warren

THE GIFT OF THE MAGI

Producer, Andre Hakim; Director, Henry King, Assistant Director, Henry Weinberger; Screenplay by Walter Bullock; Music, Alfred Newman.

CAST

Della	Jeanne Crain
Jim	Farley Granger
Santa Claus	Fred Kelsey
Menkie	Sig Ruman
Mr. Crump	Harry Hayden
Butcher	Frank Jaquet
Maurice	Fritz Feld

Jean Peters, Anne Baxter

Center: Marilyn Monroe, Charles Laughton

(PARAMOUNT)
JUST FOR YOU

Producer, Pat Duggan; Director, Elliott Nugent; Screenplay by Robert Carson; Based on "Famous" by Stephen Vincent Benet; Color by Technicolor; Choreography by Helen Tamiris; Music by Harry Warren; Lyrics by Leo Robin.

CAST

Jordan Blake	Bing Crosby
Carolina Hill	Jane Wyman
Allida de Bronkhart	Ethel Barrymore
Jerry Blake	Robert Arthur
Barbara Blake	Natalie Wood
Mrs. Angevine	Cora Witherspoon
Georgie Polansky	Ben Lessy
Hodges	Regis Toomey
Leo	Art Smith
David McKenzie	Leon Tyler
Hank Ross	Willis Bouchey
George	Herbert Vigran

Bing Crosby, Robert Arthur, Jane Wyman
Center (L. to R.) Bing Crosby, Robert Arthur; Jane Wyman, Bing Crosby
Top: Jane Wyman, Ethel Barrymore, Bing Crosby

)LUMBIA)

AFFAIR IN TRINIDAD

roducer-Director, Vincent Sherman; Screen-
by Oscar Saul and James Gunn; Story by
inia Van Upp and Berne Giler; Music by
is Stoloff and George Duning; Dances
ed by Valerie Bettis; A Beckworth Produc-

CAST

s Emery	Rita Hayworth
e Emery	Glenn Ford
Fabian	Alexander Scourby
nica	Valerie Bettis
ector Smythe	Torin Thatcher
erson	Howard Wendell
ers	Karel Stepanek
Franz Huebling	George Voskovec
ol	Steven Geray
Bronec	Walter Kohler
inique	Juanita Moore
	Gregg Martell
in	Mort Mills
	Robert Boon
ner	Ralph Moody

Rita Hayworth
Top Left: Rita Hayworth, Glenn Ford
Center: Alexander Scourby, Rita Hayworth,
Glenn Ford, Valerie Bettis
Bottom: Valerie Bettis, George Voskovec,
Rita Hayworth, Alexander Scourby

93

(WARNER BROS.)
THE CRIMSON PIRATE

Producer, Harold Hecht; Director, Rober Siodmak; Screenplay by Roland Kibbee; Col by Technicolor; Music by William Alwyn; Norma Production.

CAST

Vallo	Burt Lancas
Ojo	Nick Crav
Consuelo	Eva Bart
Humble Bellows	Torin Thatch
Prudence	James Hay
Baron Gruda	Leslie Brad
Bianca	Margot Graha
Pablo Murphy	Noel Purc
El Libre	Frederick Leices
Governor	Eliot Makeha
Colonel	Frank Petting
La Signorita	Dagmar Wyn
Attache	Christopher L

Burt Lancaster, Eva Bartok
Center: Burt Lancaster

James Hayter, Nick Cravat, Burt Lancast
Top: Nick Cravat, Eva Bartok, Burt Lanc

94

(R K O)
BEWARE, MY LOVELY

Producer, Collier Young; Director, Harry Horner; Screenplay by Mel Dinelli; Based on Story and Play "The Man" by Mel Dinelli; Music by Leith Stevens; Associate Producer, Mel Dinelli; A Filmakers Production.

CAST

Mrs. Gordon	Ida Lupino
Howard	Robert Ryan
Mr. Armstrong	Taylor Holmes
Ruth Williams	Barbara Whiting
Mr. Steven	James Willmas
Mr. Franks	O. Z. Whitehead
Grocery Boy	Dee Pollack

Robert Ryan, Barbara Whiting
Right: Taylor Holmes, Ida Lupino

(M-G-M)
THE DEVIL MAKES THREE

Producer, Richard Goldstone; Director, Andrew Marton; Assistant Director, Hermann Hohn; Screenplay by Jerry Davis; Based on Story by Lawrence Bachmann.

CAST

Capt. Jeff Eliot	Gene Kelly
Wilhelmina Lehrt	Pier Angeli
Col. James Terry	Richard Rober
Lt. Parker	Richard Egan
Heisemann	Claus Clausen
Hansig	Wilfried Seyferth
Cabaret Singer	Margot Hielscher
Mrs. Keigler	Annie Rosar
Sgt. at Airport	Harold Benedict
Mr. Nolder	Otto Gebuhr
Mrs. Nolder	Gertrude Wolle

and Heinrich Gretler, Charlotte Flemming, Charles Gordon Howard, Bum Kruger, Claus Benton Lombard, Ivan Petrovich, Sepp Rist, Michael Tellering.

Pier Angeli, Gene Kelly
Right: Richard Egan, Michael Tellering, Gene Kelly

97

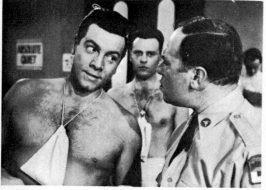

Mario Lanza

(M-G-M)

BECAUSE YOU'RE MINE

Producer, Joe Pasternak; Director, Alexan
Hall; Screenplay by Karl Tunberg and Leona
Spigelgass; Based on Story by Ruth Broc
Flippen and Sy Gomberg; Musical Directi
Johnny Green; Color by Technicolor.

CAST

Renaldo Rossano_____Mario Lan
Bridget Batterson_____Doretta Morr
Sgt. Batterson_____James Whitmc
Ben Jones_____Dean Mil
Francesca Landers_____Paula Cord
Patty Ware_____Jeff Donn
Mrs. Montville_____Spring Byingt
Gen. Montville_____Curtis Cooks
Capt. Loring_____Don Por
Albert Parkson Foster_____Eduard Fra
Artie Pilcer_____Bobby V
Horsey_____Ralph Re
Mrs. Rossano_____Celia Lovs
Maestro Paradori_____Alexander Stein

(M-G-M)

Center: Mario Lanza, William Phillips
Top: Mario Lanza, James Whitmore, Jeff Donnell, Doretta Morrow
Right: Doretta Morrow, Mario Lanza, James Whitmore

(UNITED ARTISTS)

THE THIEF

Producer, Clarence Greene; Director, Russell Rouse; Screenplay by Clarence Greene and Russell Rouse; Music by Herschel Gilbert; A Harry M. Popkin Production.

CAST

Allan Fields	Ray Milland
Mr. Bleek	Martin Gabel
The Girl	Rita Gam
Harris	Harry Bronson
Dr. Linstrum	John McKutcheon
Miss Philips	Rita Vale
Beal	Rex O'Malley
Walters	Joe Conlin

Rita Vale, Harry Bronson
Center: Ray Milland
Top: Rita Gam, Ray Milland

Rita Gam
Top: Martin Gabel, Ray Milland

(UNIVERSAL)
BACK AT THE FRONT

Producer, Leonard Goldstein, Director, George Sherman; Screenplay by Lou Breslow, Don McGuire and Oscar Brodney; Story by Lou Breslow and Don McGuire; Based on Characters Created by Bill Mauldin; Assistant Director, Tom Shaw.

CAST

Willie	Tom Ewell
Joe	Harvey Lembeck
Nida	Mari Blanchard
Sgt. Rose	Richard Long
Capt. White	Palmer Lee
Gen. Dixon	Barry Kelley
Johnny Redondo	Russell Johnson
Maj. Ormsby	Vaughn Taylor
Ben	Aram Katcher
Pete Wilson	George Ramsey
Sameko	Aen-Ling Chow
Rickshaw Boy	Benson Fong

Palmer Lee, Tom Ewell, Harvey Lembe

MY MAN AND I

Producer, Stephen Ames; Director, William A. Wellman; Screenplay by John Fante and Jack Leonard; Music by David Buttolph; Assistant Director, George Rhein.

CAST

Nancy	Shelley Winters
Chu Chu Ramirez	Ricardo Montalban
Ansel Ames	Wendell Corey
Mrs. Ansel Ames	Claire Trevor
Sheriff	Robert Burton
Manuel Ramirez	Jose Torvay
Celestino Garcia	Jack Elam
Willie Chung	Pasqual Garcia Pena
Frankie	George Chandler
Vincente Aguilar	Juan Torena
Joe Mendacio	Carlos Conde

George Chandler, Ricardo Montalban
Shelley Winters

(20th CENTURY-FOX)
MY WIFE'S BEST FRIEND

Producer, Robert Bassler; Director, Richard Sale; Assistant Director, Hal Klein; Screenplay by Isobel Lennart; Based on Story by John Briard Harding; Music, Leigh Harline.

CAST

Virginia Mason	Anne Baxter
George Mason	Macdonald Carey
Rev. Chamberlain	Cecil Kellaway
Pete Bentham	Casey Adams
Jane Richards	Catherine McLeod
Nicholas Reed	Leif Erickson
Mrs. Chamberlain	Frances Bavier
Flossy Chamberlain	Mary Sullivan
Buddy Chamberlain	Martin Milner
Katie	Billie Bird
Mike	Michael Ross
Dr. McCarran	Morgan Farley
Hannah	Ann Staunton
Walter Rogers	Emmett Vogan

and Wild Red Berry, Henry Kulky, John Hedloe, John McKee, Phil Hartman, Junius Matthews, Joe Haworth, Ed Dearing.

Anne Baxter, Macdonald Carey

Charles Chaplin in
"Limelight"

Charles Chaplin, Jr., Charles Chaplin, Wheeler Dryden, André Eglevsky, Claire Bloom
Top Left: Claire Bloom, Charles Chaplin
Top Right: Marjorie Bennett, Charles Chaplin

(UNITED ARTISTS)

LIMELIGHT

Producer-Director, Charles Chaplin; Screenplay by Charles Chaplin; Music by Charles Chaplin; Assistant Director, Robert Aldrich.

CAST

Calvero .... Charles Chaplin
Terry .... Claire Bloom
Neville .... Sydney Chaplin

For The Ballet

Harlequin .... Andre Eglevsky
Columbine .... Melissa Hayden
Clowns ...... Charles Chaplin, Charles Chaplin, Jr., Wheeler Dryden
Cast: Nigel Bruce, Norman Lloyd, Buster Keaton, Marjorie Bennett

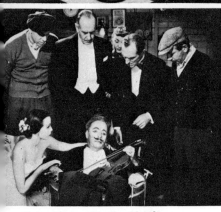

Claire Bloom, Charles Chaplin

Norman Lloyd, Sydney Chaplin, Claire Bloom

Center: Buster Keaton, Charles Chaplin
Top: Charles Chaplin

(PARAMOUNT)

SOMEBODY LOVES ME

Producers, William Perlberg and Geo
Seaton; Director, Irving Brecher; Screenplay
Irving Brecher; Suggested by careers of Bloss
Seeley and Benny Fields; Color by Technicol

CAST

Blossom Seeley	Betty Hutt
Benny Fields	Ralph Meel
Sam Doyle	Robert Ke
Nola Beech	Adele Jerg
Essie	Billie B
Forrest	Henry Sl
Lake	Sid Tom
D. J. Grauman	Ludwig Stos

Robert Keith, Betty Hutton, Ralph Meeker
Top: Betty Hutton, Ralph Meeker

Ralph Meeker, Henry Slate, Betty Hutt
Sid Tomak

(20th CENTURY-FOX)

WAY OF A GAUCHO

Producer, Philip Dunne; Associate Produc
Joseph C. Behm; Director, Jacques Tourne
Screenplay by Philip Dunne; Based on No
by Herbert Childs; Color by Technicol
Music, Alfred Newman, Sol Kaplan.

CAST

Martin	Rory Calho
Teresa	Gene Tier
Salinas	Richard Bo
Miguel	Hugh Marl
Falcon	Everett Slo
Father Fernandez	Enrique Cha
Valverde	Jorge Villo
Julio	Roland Dur
Tia Maria	Lidia Cam

and Hugo Mancini, Nester Yoan, Raoul As
John Paris, Alex Peters, John Henchley, I
Dillon, Lia Centeno, Claudio Tores, Anth
Ugrin, Douglas Poole, Mario Abdah, Te
Acosta, Oscar Lucero.

Enrique Chaica, Rory Calhoun, Gene Tierney
Center: Gene Tierney, Rory Calhoun
Right: Rory Calhoun, Richard Boone

106

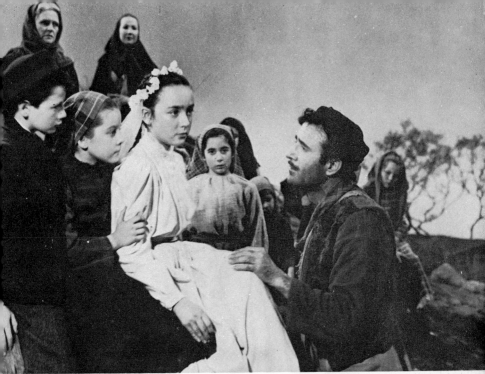

(WARNER BROS.)
THE MIRACLE OF FATIMA

Producer, Bryan Foy; Director, John Brahm; Assistant Director, James McMahon; Screenplay by Cran Wilbur and James O'Hanlon; Music by Max Steiner; Color by WarnerColor.

CAST

Hugo Da Silva	Gilbert Roland
Maria Rosa	Angela Clark
Arturo Dos Santos	Frank Silvera
Antonio	Jay Novello
Father Ferreira	Richard Hale
Manuel Marto	Norman Rice
Olimpia	Frances Morris
Magistrate	Carl Millitaire
Lucia Dos Santos	Susan Whitney
Jacinta Marto	Sherry Jackson
Francisco Marto	Sammy Ogg

Gilbert Roland

Top: Sammy Ogg, Sherry Jackson, Susan Whitney, Gilbert Roland
Right: Paul Fierro, Susan Whitney, Sammy Ogg, Richard Hale, Sherry Jackson

Alexis Smith, William Holden

(PARAMOUNT)
THE TURNING POINT

Producer, Irving Asher; Director, Willi Dieterle; Screenplay by Warren Duff; Based Story by Horace McCoy.

CAST

Jerry McKibbon	William Hol
John Conroy	Edmond O'B
Amanda Waycross	Alexis Sm
Matt Conroy	Tom T
Eichelberger	Ed Be
Ackerman	Dan Day
Carmelina	Adele Longm
Clint	Ray
Harrigan	Ted DeCo
Joe Silbray	Don Po
Fogel	Howard Freer
Red	Neville Br

George Brent, Jane Russell

(R K O)
MONTANA BELLE

Producer, Howard Welsch; Associate ducer, Robert Peters; Director, Allan Dw Screenplay by Horace McCoy and Normar Hall; Story by M. Coates Webster and How Welsch; Music by Nathan Scott; Color by T nicolor.

CAST

Belle Starr	Jane Ru
Tom Bradfield	George B
Bob	Scott B
Mac	Forrest Tu
Pete Bivins	Andy De
Ringo	Jack Lam
Towner	John I
Emmett Dalton	Ray
Grat	Rory Malli
Jim Clark	Roy Bar
Ben	Holly
Bank Clerk	Ned Daven
Rideout	Dick E
Ripple	Eugene
Combs	Stanley And

Steve Cochran, Cornel Wilde, Phyllis Thaxter, Karl Malden

(WARNER BROS.)
OPERATION SECRET

Producer, Henry Blanke; Director, Lewis er; Assistant Director, William Kissel; Scr play by James R. Webb and Harold Medf Story by Alvin Josephy and John Twist; gested by Lt. Col. Peter Ortiz; Music by Webb.

CAST

Peter Forrester	Cornel W
Sgt. Marcel Brevoort	Steve Coc
Maria	Phyllis Tha
Major Latrec	Karl Ma
Capt. Armand	Paul Pic
Mr. Robbins	Lester Matt
Lt. Duncan	Dan O'He
Herr Bauer	Jay No
Capt. Chiron	Wilton C
German Sergeant	Dan
Capt. Hughes	William Leic
Monk	Tom Browne H
Zabreski	Philip

and Harlan Warde, Kenneth Patterson, G Kellogg, Wayne Taylor, Claude Dunkin, liam Slack.

UNDER THE RED SEA

ns Hass Production; Narrative and Pro-
Supervision by Bill Park; Narrator, Les
ne; Music by Bert Grund.

CAST

ion Leader	Dr. Hans Hass
ion Secretary	Lottie Berl
ion Members	Gerald Weidler, Leo
hrer, Edward Wawrowetz, Alfonso Hoch-	
user (Xenophon)	
se Recruits	

AMOUNT)

THE SAVAGE

ucer, Mel Epstein; Director, George
l; Screenplay by Sydney Boehm; Based
el by L. L. Foreman; Color by Techni-
Music by Paul Sawtell.

CAST

nnet	Charlton Heston
lathersall	Susan Morrow
ston Hathersall	Peter Hanson
	Joan Taylor
rnold Vaugant	Richard Rober
g Dog	Donald Porter
east	Ted De Corsia
Eagle	Ian MacDonald
artin	Milburn Stone
i	Angela Clarke
er Aherne	Orley Lindgren
fane	Larry Tolan
llis	Howard Negley
orris	Frank Richards
Thunder	John Miljan

Charlton Heston, Joan Taylor

CENTURY-FOX)

PONY SOLDIER

ucer, Samuel G. Engel; Director, Joseph
wman; Assistant Director, Horace Hough;
olay by John C. Higgins; Based on Story
rnett Weston; Color by Technicolor;
Alex North.

CAST

a MacDonald	Tyrone Power
	Cameron Mitchell
	Thomas Gomez
d	Penny Edwards
alhoun	Robert Horton
Running	Anthony Earl Numkena
Moon	Adeline DeWalt Reynolds
or Frazer	Howard Petrie
g Bear	Stuart Randall
Neeley	Richard Shackleton
ames Hayward, Muriel Landers, Frank	
va, Louis Heminger, Grady Galloway,	
C. Strongheart, Chalos Loya, Anthony	
na, Sr., John War Eagle, Chief Bright-	
hunder-Sky.	

Thomas Gomez, Tyrone Power, Cameron Mitchell

Richard Lightner, Guinn Williams, Gary Cooper

Dick Paxton, Sarah Selby, Alan Lad
Richard Carlyle

(WARNER BROS)

SPRINGFIELD RIFLE

Producer, Louis F. Edelman; Director, Andre DeToth; Assistant Director, Frank Mattison; Screenplay by Charles Marquis Warren and Frank Davis; Based on Story by Sloan Nibley; Color by WarnerColor.

CAST

Maj. Lex Kearny	Gary Cooper
Erin Kearny	Phyllis Thaxter
Austin "Mac" McCool	David Brian
Lt. Col. Hudson	Paul Kelly
Pete Elm	Lon Chaney
Capt. Edward Tennick	Philip Carey
Matthew Quint	James Millican
Sgt. Snow	G. "Big Boy" Williams
Mizzell	Alan Hale, Jr.
Pvt. Ferguson	James Brown
Lt. Evans	Jerry O'Sullivan
Sgt. Poole	Ned Young

and Martin Milner, Wilton Graff, Richard Hale, Vince Barnett, Poodles Hanneford, Jack Woody, William Fawcett.

(WARNER BROS.)

THE IRON MISTRESS

Producer, Henry Blanke; Director, Gor Douglas; Assistant Director, Oren Hagl Screenplay by James R. Webb; Based on N by Paul I. Wellman; Music by Max Stei Color by Technicolor.

CAST

Jim Bowie	Alan L
Judalon de Bornay	Virginia M
Juan Moreno	Joseph Ca
Ursula de Veramendi	Phyllis
Philippe de Cabanal	Alf Kj
Narcisse de Bornay	Douglas
"Bloody Jack" Sturdevant	Tony Ca
Henri Contrecourt	Ned Yo
James Audubon	George Vosk
Rezin Bowie	Richard Ca
General Cuny	Robert Emh

and Donald Beddoe, Harold Gordon, Gor Nelson, Jay Novello, Nick Dennis, Sarah Se Dick Paxton, George Lewis, Edward Colm Daria Massey.

Lon Chaney, Gary Cooper, Paul Kelly
Center: Phyllis Thaxter, Gary Cooper

Alan Ladd, Virginia Mayo, Richard Carl
Center: Alan Ladd, Ramsey Hill, Fred Ca
Douglas Dick

ncer Tracy

Lloyd Bridges, Spencer Tracy, Van Johnson,
John Dehner

Van Johnson

n McGiveney

(M-G-M)
PLYMOUTH ADVENTURE

Producer, Dore Schary; Director, Clarence
Brown; Screenplay by Helen Deutsch; Based
on Novel by Ernest Gebler; Music by Miklos Rozsa;
Color by Technicolor.

CAST

Capt. Christopher Jones	Spencer Tracy
Dorothy Bradford	Gene Tierney
John Alden	Van Johnson
William Bradford	Leo Genn
Coppin	Lloyd Bridges
Priscilla Mullins	Dawn Addams
William Brewster	Barry Jones
Miles Standish	Noel Drayton
Gilbert Winslow	John Dehner
William Button	Tommy Ivo
Edward Winslow	Lowell Gilmore

and Rhys Williams, Damian O'Flynn, Keith
McConnell, Elizabeth Harrower, Owen McGive-
ney, Paul Cavanagh, Ivis Goulding, Murray
Matheson, Elizabeth Flournoy, Kathleen Lock-
hart, David Sober, Roger Broaddus, Hugh Pryse,
James Logan, Gene Coogan, Kay English, Matt
Moore, John Dierkes.

Leo Genn

yd Bridges

att Moore

Spencer Tracy, Gene Tierney

Lowell Gilmore

Barry Jones

(20th CENTURY-FOX)

BLOODHOUNDS
OF BROADWAY

Producer, George Jessel; Director, Ha□
Jones; Assistant Director, Stanley Ho□
Screenplay by Sy Gomberg; Adaptation by
bert Mannheimer; Color by Technicolor; M
by Eliot Daniel, Ben Oakland and □
Webster.

CAST

Emily Ann Stackerlee	Mitzi Ga
Robert "Numbers" Foster	Scott B
Tessie Sammis	Mitzi G
Yvonne	Marguerite Chap
Inspector McNamara	Michael O'□
Poorly Sammis	Wally Ve
Dave, The Dude	Henry □
Ropes McGonigle	George E. S
Lookout Louie	Edwin
Curtaintime Charlie	Richard A

and Sharon Baird, Ralph Volkie, Charles B□
inski, Timothy Carey, Bill Walker, Paul V
ler, Alfred Mizner, Emile Meyer.

Left: Wally Vernon, Scott Brady, Mitzi G
Top: Richard Allan, Mitzi Gaynor, Mitzi □

(UNIVERSAL)

IT GROWS ON TREES

Producer, Leonard Goldstein; Direc
Arthur Lubin; Assistant Director, John S□
wood; Story and Screenplay by Leonard P□
kins and Barney Slater; Music by Frank Skin□

CAST

Polly Baxter	Irene Du□
Phil Baxter	Dean Jag□
Diane Baxter	Joan Ev□
Ralph Bowen	Richard Cre□
Mrs. Pryor	Edith Me□
Midge Baxter	Sandy Desc□
Flip Baxter	Dee Poll□
Finlay Murchison	Les Trema□
Henry Carrollman	Malcolm Lee Be□
Dr. Harold Burrows	Forrest Le□
John Letherby	Frank Fergu□
McGurie	Bob Swee□

Dean Jagger, Richard Crenna, Joan Evans,
Irene Dunne
Center: Irene Dunne, Dean Jagger

112

Dean Jagger, Sandy Descher, Dee Poll□

(R K O)
FACE TO FACE

Producer, Huntington Hartford; Associate Producers, George Tobin and Norman A. Manning; Music by Hugo Friedhofer.

THE SECRET SHARER

Director, John Brahm; Assistant Director, Frank Heath; From the Story by Joseph Conrad; Screenplay by Aeneas MacKenzie.

CAST

The Captain	James Mason
The Swimmer	Michael Pate
Capt. Archbold	Gene Lockhart
1st Mate	Albert Sharpe
2nd Mate	Sean McClory
Ship's Cook	Alec Harford

THE BRIDE COMES TO YELLOW SKY

Director, Bretaigne Windust; Assistant Director, Frank Heath; Screenplay by James Agee; From the Story by Stephen Crane.

CAST

The Sheriff	Robert Preston
The Bride	Marjorie Steele
The Bad Man	Minor Watson
The Drummer	Dan Seymour
The Saloon Keeper	Olive Carey
The Prisoner	James Agee
Ed	Gayle Kellogg

Left: Michael Pate, James Mason
Top: Marjorie Steele, Robert Preston

(UNIVERSAL)
BECAUSE OF YOU

Producer, Albert J. Cohen; Director, Joseph Pevney; Assistant Directors, Frank Shaw and James Welch; Screenplay by Ketti Frings; Story by Thelma Robinson; Music by Frank Skinner.

CAST

Christine Carroll	Loretta Young
Steve Kimberly	Jeff Chandler
Mike Monroe	Alex Nicol
Susan Arnold	Frances Dee
Dr. Breen	Alexander Scourby
Rosemary Balder	Lynne Roberts
Peachie	Mae Clark
Kim	Gayle Reed
George	Billy Wayne
Judy	Frances Karath

Alex Nicol, Loretta Young

113

Kurt Kasznar, Charles Boyer, Bobby Driscoll, Marsha Hunt, Louis Jourdan

(COLUMBIA)

THE HAPPY TIME

Louis Jourdan, Marcel Dalio, Charles Boyer, W
Wright, Marsha Hunt, Kurt Kasznar, Linda Ch
tian; Center (L. to R.): Louis Jourdan, Linda
Christian; Charles Boyer, Bobby Driscoll

Robert Coote, Stewart Granger, Louis Calhern, Deborah Kerr

(M-G-M)

THE PRISONER OF ZENDA

Producer, Pandro S. Berman; Director, Richard Thorpe; Screenplay by John L. Balderston and Noel Langley; Adaptation by Wells Root from the Novel by Anthony Hope and the Dramatization by Edward Rose; Music by Alfred Newman; Adapted by Conrad Salinger; Color by Technicolor.

CAST

Rudolf Rassendyll	Stewart Granger
King Rudolf V	Stewart Granger
Princess Flavia	Deborah Kerr
Col. Zapt	Louis Calhern
Antoinette De Mauban	Jane Greer
The Cardinal	Lewis Stone
Michael, Duke of Strelsau	Robert Douglas
Fritz Von Tarlenheim	Robert Coote
Johann	Peter Brocco
Josef	Francis Pierlot
Rupert of Hentzau	James Mason

Mason, Robert Coote, Louis Calhern, Stewart Granger
Center: Robert Douglas, Jane Greer, James Mason
Right: Stewart Granger in dual role

(20th CENTURY-FOX)
NIGHT WITHOUT SLEEP

Producer, Robert Bassler; Director, Roy Baker; Screenplay by Frank Partos and Elick Moll; Story by Elick Moll; Music, Cyril Mockridge, Alfred Newman, Ken Darby and Haven Gillespie.

CAST
Julie Bannon............Linda Darnell
Richard Morton............Gary Merrill
Lisa Muller............Hildegarde Neff
Laura Harkness............Joyce MacKenzie
Emily Morton............June Vincent
Dr. Clarke............Donald Randolph
John Harkness............Hugh Beaumont
Mrs. Carter............Louise Lorimer
Mr. Carter............William Forrest
George............Steven Geray
Singer............Mauri Lynn
Henry............Bill Walker
Maid............Mae Marsh
Benny............Ben Carter

Gary Merrill, Hildegarde Neff

(PARAMOUNT)
THE BLAZING FOREST

Producers, William H. Pine and William C. Thomas; Director, Edward Ludwig; Screenplay by Lewis R. Foster and Winston Miller; Color by Technicolor; Music by Lucien Cailliet.

CAST
Kelly Hanson............John Payne
Syd Jessup............William Demarest
Jessie Crain............Agnes Moorehead
Joe Morgan............Richard Arlen
Sharon Wilks............Susan Morrow
Beans............Roscoe Ates
Grace............Lynne Roberts
Ranger............Ewing Mitchell
Max............Walter Reed
Lumberjacks....Jim Davis, Joey Ray, Joe Garcia, Brett Houston, Max Wagner.

John Payne, Richard Arlen

(COLUMBIA)
PRINCE OF PIRATES

Producer, Sam Katzman; Director, Sidney Salkow; Assistant Director, Jack Corrick; Story by William Copeland and Herbert Kline; Screenplay by John O'Dea and Samuel Newman; Color by Technicolor.

CAST
Prince Roland............John Derek
Nita Orde............Barbara Rush
Princess Maria............Carla Balenda
Stephan............Whitfield Connor
Count Blanco............Edgar Barrier
Treeg............Robert Shayne
Jan............Harry Lauter
Koepke............Don Harvey
Greb............Henry Rowland
Brenner............Glase Lohman
Capt. Brock............Gene Roth
Carl............Bob Peoples
Meyers............Sandy Sanders
Gen. DuBois............Joseph F. McGuinn
Lund............Al Cantor
Spanish Admiral............Edward Colmans

Carla Balenda, Barbara Rush, John Derek Whitfield Connor

onar Colleano, Arthur Franz, Lee Marvin,
Nick Dennis

(COLUMBIA)

EIGHT IRON MEN

Producer, Stanley Kramer; Associate Producers, Edna and Edward Anhalt; Director, Edward Dmytryk; Assistant Director, James Nicholson; Screenplay by Harry Brown; Adapted from his Play "A Sound of Hunting"; Music by Leith Stevens.

CAST

Collucci	Bonar Colleano
Carter	Arthur Franz
Mooney	Lee Marvin
Coke	Richard Kiley
Sapiros	Nick Dennis
Ferguson	James Griffith
Muller	Dick Moore
Small	George Cooper
Capt. Trelawny	Barney Phillips
Walsh	Robert Nichols
Lt. Crane	Richard Grayson
Hunter	Douglas Henderson
Girl	Mary Castle
Cafferty	David McMahon

Cleo Moore, Hugo Haas, Mark Andrews

(COLUMBIA)

STRANGE FASCINATION

Written, Produced and Directed by Hugo Haas; Assistant Director, Leonard J. Shapiro; Music by Vaclav Divina and Jacob Gimpel; Associate Producer, Robert Erlik.

CAST

Margo	Cleo Moore
Paul Marvan	Hugo Haas
Diana	Mona Barrie
Carlo	Rick Vallin
June	Karen Sharpe
Shiner	Marc Krah
Yvette	Genevieve Aumont
Walter	Patrick Holmes
Mary	Maura Murphy
Douglas	Brian O'Hara
Investigator	Anthony Jochim

and Dr. Ross Tompson, Maria Bibikoff, Gayne Whitman, Roy Engel, Robert Knapp.

Dawn Addams, Peter Lawford, Derek Bond

(M-G-M)

THE HOUR OF 13

Producer, Hayes Goetz; Director, Harold French; Screenplay by Leon Gordon and Howard Emmett Rogers; Based on Novel by Philip MacDonald; Music by John Addison.

CAST

Nicholas Revel	Peter Lawford
Jane Frensham	Dawn Addams
Connor	Roland Culver
Sir Christopher Lenhurst	Derek Bond
Ernie Perker	Leslie Dwyer
Sir Herbert Frensham	Michael Hordern
MacStreet	Colin Gordon
Mrs. Chumley Orr	Heather Thatcher
Ford	Jack McNaughton
Mr. Chumley Orr	Campbell Cotts
Lady Elmbridge	Fabia Drake
Anderson	Michael Goodliffe
Magistrate	Moultrie Kelsall
Cummings	Peter Copley
The Terror	Richard Shaw

Clifton Webb, Debra Paget, Robert Wagner

Roy Roberts, Robert Wagner, Clifton Webb
Center: Ruth Hussey, Clifton Webb
Right: Clifton Webb

118

(20th CENTURY-FOX)

STARS AND STRIPES FOREVER

Producer, Lamar Trotti; Director, Henry Koster; Assistant Director, Eli Dunn; Screenplay by Lamar Trotti; Screen Story by Ernest Vajda; Based on "Marching Along" by John Philip Sousa; Color by Technicolor; Choreography, Al White, Jr.

CAST

John Philip Sousa	Clifton Webb
Lily	Debra Paget
Willie	Robert Wagner
Jennie	Ruth Hussey
Col. Randolph	Finlay Currie
Mme. Bernsdorff-Mueller	Benay Venuta
Major Houston	Roy Roberts
David Blakely	Tom Browne Henry
Mr. Pickering	Lester Matthews
Maid	Maude Prickett
Organ Grinder	Erno Verebes
Secretary of The Navy	Richard Garrick
Music Professor	Romo Vincent
President Harrison	Roy Gordon

and Florence Shirley, Delos Jewkes, Norman Leavitt, Hellen Van Tuyl, Walter Woolf King, Roger Moore, Thomas E. Jackson, Maude Wallace, Lenee Martin, Sharon Jan Altman, Nicholas Koster, William Vedder, Olan Soule, Aileen Carlyle, Jack Rice, Paul Maxey, Frank Ferguson.

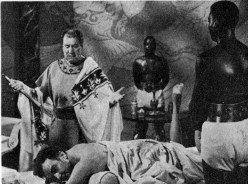

Victor Mature, Jean Simmons, Alan Young
Right: Maurice Evans, Alan Mowbray
Top Right: Alan Young

(R K O)
ANDROCLES AND THE LION

Producer, Gabriel Pascal; Director, Chester Erskine; Screenplay adapted by Chester Erskine and Ken Englund; Based on Play by Bernard Shaw; Music by Frederick Hollander.

CAST

Lavinia	Jean Simmons
Androcles	Alan Young
Captain	Victor Mature
Ferrovius	Robert Newton
Caesar	Maurice Evans
Megaera	Elsa Lanchester
Lentulus	Reginald Gardiner
Menagerie Keeper	Gene Lockhart
Editor	Alan Mowbray
Spintho	Noel Willman
Cato	John Hoyt
Centurian	Jim Backus
Metellus	Lowell Gilmore

John Hoyt, Jean Simmons, Alan Young

Center (L. to R.): Maurice Evans, Alan Young, Jean Simmons, Victor Mature

(M-G-M)
SKY FULL OF MOON

Producer, Sidney Franklin, Jr.; Direction and Screenplay by Norman Foster; Assistant Director, Arvid Griffen; Music by Paul Sawtell.

CAST

Harley Williams	Carleton Carpenter
Dixie Delmar	Jan Sterling
Al	Keenan Wynn
Customer	Robert Burton
Change Girl	Elaine Stewart
Otis	Emmett Lynn
Rodeo Official	Douglass Dumbrille
Balladeers	Jonathan Cott and Sheb Wooley

Robert Burton, Carleton Carpenter, Jan Ste Keenan Wynn

(20th CENTURY-FOX)
MY PAL GUS

Producer, Stanley Rubin; Director, Robert Parrish; Assistant Director, J. Richard Maybery; Written by Fay and Michael Kanin; Music, Leigh Harline.

CAST

Dave Jennings	Richard Widmark
Lydia Marble	Joanne Dru
Joyce	Audrey Totter
Gus Jennings	George Winslow
Ivy Tolliver	Joan Banks
Farley Norris	Regis Toomey
Karl	Ludwig Donath
Polly Pahlman	Ann Morrison
Anna	Lisa Golm
Tommy	Christopher Olsen
Mr. Evans	Robert Foulk
Judy	Mimi Gibson

and Sandy Descher, Marie Brown, Gordon Nelson, Mabel Albertson, Jerrilyn Flannery, William Cottrell, Jay Adler, Frank Marlowe, Franklyn Farnum, William Dyer, Jr., Otto Forrest, James Flavin, Jonathan Hale, Frank Nelson.

George Winslow, Richard Widmark

(UNIVERSAL)
THE BLACK CASTLE

Producer, William Alland; Director, Nathan Juran; Assistant Director, William Holland; Story and Screenplay by Jerry Sackheim; Dance Director, Harold Belfer.

CAST

Count Von Bruno	Stephen McNally
Richard Beckett	Richard Greene
Elga	Paula Corday
Dr. Meissen	Boris Karloff
Gargon	Lon Chaney, Jr.
Herr Von Melcher	Michael Pate
Romley	Tudor Owen
Krantz	Otto Waldis
Herr Stieken	John Hoyt
Fender	Henry Corden

Richard Green, Michael Pate, John Hoyt Lon Chaney

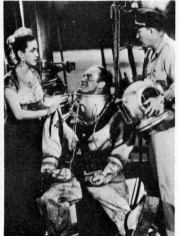

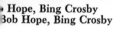
Hope, Bing Crosby
Bob Hope, Bing Crosby

Dorothy Lamour, Bob Hope,
Bing Crosby

Bing Crosby, Bob Hope
Top: Bob Hope, Dorothy
Lamour, Bing Crosby

Dorothy Lamour, Bob Hope

(PARAMOUNT)

ROAD TO BALI

Producer, Harry Tugend; Director, Hal Walker; Screenplay by Frank Butler, Hal Kanter and William Morrow; Story by Frank Butler and Harry Tugend; Color by Technicolor; Musical Numbers Staged by Charles O'Curran; Lyrics by Johnny Burke; Music by James Van Heusen.

CAST

Harold Gridley	Bob Hope
George Cochran	Bing Crosby
Lalah	Dorothy Lamour
Ken Arok	Murvyn Vye
Gung	Peter Coe
Bhoma Da	Ralph Moody
Ramayana	Leon Askin

Joan Fontaine, Emlyn Williams, Finlay C
George Sanders, Robert Douglas
Top: Robert Taylor

Robert Taylor, Elizabeth Taylor
Top: George Sanders, Robert Taylor

George Sanders, Elizabeth Taylor,
Guy Rolfe (extreme right)
Center: Robert Douglas, George Sander
Robert Taylor

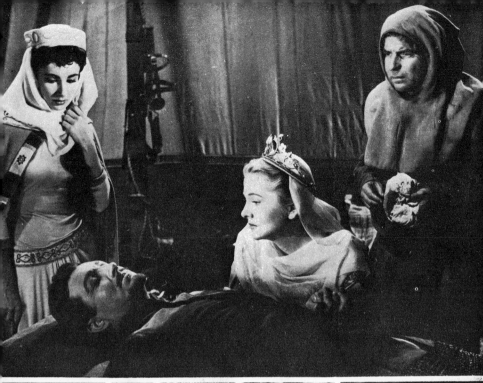

(M-G-M)

IVANHOE

Producer, Pandro S. Berman; Director, Richard Thorpe; Screenplay by Noel Langley; Adaptation by Aeneas MacKenzie; Based on Novel by Sir Walter Scott; Music by Miklos Rozsa; Color by Technicolor.

CAST

Ivanhoe	Robert Taylor
Rebecca	Elizabeth Taylor
Rowena	Joan Fontaine
De Bois-Guilbert	George Sanders
Wamba	Emlyn Williams
Sir Hugh De Bracy	Robert Douglas
Cedric	Finlay Currie
Isaac	Felix Aylmer
Font De Boeuf	Francis DeWolff
Prince John	Guy Rolfe
King Richard	Norman Wooland
Waldemar Fitzurse	Basil Sydney
Locksley	Harold Warrender

and Patrick Holt, Roderick Lovell, Sebastian Cabot, John Ruddock, Michael Brennan, Megs Jenkins, Valentine Dyall, Lionel Harris, Carl Jaffe.

eorge Sanders
(L. to R.): Joan
ne, Robert Taylor,
izabeth Taylor

Emlyn Williams; (Top):
Elizabeth Taylor, Robert
Taylor, Joan Fontaine,
Emlyn Williams

(M-G-M)
MILLION DOLLAR MERMAID

Producer, Arthur Hornblow, Jr.; Director, Mervyn LeRoy; Screenplay by Everett Freeman; Underwater Choreography by Audrene Brier; Color by Technicolor.

CAST

Annette Kellerman	Esther Williams
James Sullivan	Victor Mature
Frederick Kellerman	Walter Pidgeon
Alfred Harper	David Brian
Annette (at 10)	Donna Corcoran
Doc Cronnol	Jesse White
Pavlova	Maria Tallchief
Aldrich	Howard Freeman
Policeman	Charles Watts
Garvey	Wilton Graff
Prosecutor	Frank Ferguson
Judge	James Bell
Conductor	James Flavin
Director	Willis Bouchey

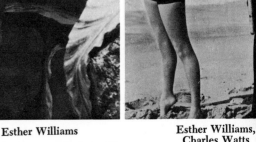

Esther Williams, Victor Mature

Esther Williams

Esther Williams, Charles Watts

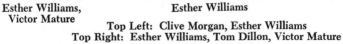
Top Left: Clive Morgan, Esther Williams
Top Right: Esther Williams, Tom Dillon, Victor Mature

124

(R K O)
HANS CHRISTIAN ANDERSEN

Producer, Samuel Goldwyn; Director, Charles Vidor; Screenplay by Moss Hart; Based on Story by Myles Connolly; Words and Music by Frank Loesser; Choreography by Roland Petit; Color by Technicolor.

CAST

Hans Christian Andersen	Danny Kaye
Niels	Farley Granger
Doro	Jeanmaire
Peter	Joey Walsh
Otto	Philip Tonge
The Hussar	Erik Bruhn
The Prince in the Ballet	Roland Petit
Schoolmaster	John Brown
Burgomaster	John Qualen
Celine	Jeanne Lafayette
Stage Doorman	Robert Malcolm
Farmer	George Chandler
1st Gendarme	Fred Kelsey
2nd Gendarme	Gil Perkins
Lars	Peter Votrian

y Walsh, Danny Kaye

Jeanmaire, Danny Kay

Danny Kaye

Top (L. to R.): Farley Granger, Jeanmaire; Danny Kaye, Jeanmaire, Farley Granger; Jeanmaire, Danny Kaye

UNIVERSAL)
AGAINST ALL FLAGS

Producer, Howard Christie; Director, George Sherman; Assistant Directors, John Sherwood, Phil Bowles and James Welch; Screenplay by Aeneas MacKenzie and Joseph Hoffman; Story by Aeneas MacKenzie; Music by Hans J. Salter; Color by Technicolor.

CAST

Brian Hawks	Errol Flynn
Spitfire Stevens	Maureen O'Hara
Capt. Roc Brasiliano	Anthony Quinn
Princess Patma	Alice Kelley
Molvina MacGregor	Mildred Natwick
Jones	John Tully
Harris	John Alderson
Gow	Harry Cording
Swaine	Michael Ross
Crop-Ear	Paul Newlan

Right: Anthony Quinn, Errol Flynn, Maureen O'Hara
Top: Errol Flynn, Anthony Quinn

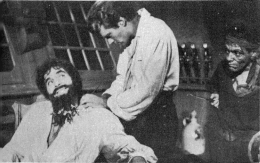

(R K O)
BLACKBEARD, THE PIRATE

Producer, Edmund Grainger; Director, Rao Walsh; Assistant Director, James Casey; Scree play by Alan LeMay; Story by DeVallon Sco Color by Technicolor; Music by Victor Youn An Edmund Grainger Production.

CAST

Blackbeard	Robert Newt
Edwina	Linda Darn
Worley	William Benc
Maynard	Keith And
Sir Henry Morgan	Torin Thatch
Alvina	Irene Ry
Noll	Alan Mowbi
Briggs	Richard Eg
Gilly	Skelton Knag
Dutchman	Dick Wes
Pierre La Garde	Anthony Caru
Tom Whetstone	Jack Lambe
Jeremy	Noel Drayt
Job Maggot	Pat Flahe

William Bendix, Linda Darnell. Keith Andes, Irene Ryan

Center (L. to R.): Robert Newton, Keith Andes, Skelton Knaggs; Keith Andes, Robert Newton, Skelton Knaggs

(BRANDON)
JULIUS CAESAR
Producer-Director, David Bradley; Screenplay by William Shakespeare; Music by John Becker; An Avon Production.

CAST

Julius Caesar................................Harold Tasker
Octavius Caesar............................Robert Holt
Marcus Antonius..........................Charlton Heston
Emil Lepidus................................Theodore Cloak
Brutus.......................................David Bradley
Cassius......................................Grosvenor Glenn
Casca.......................................William Russell
Decius......................................Frederick Roscoe
Cinna.......................................Arthur Sus
Popilius....................................Cornelius Peeples
Flavius.....................................Alfred Edyvean
Marullus....................................John O'Leary
Artemidorus................................Homer Dietmeier
Soothsayer.................................Don Walker
Cinna the Poet............................Russell Gruebner
Strato......................................George Gilbert
Lucius......................................George Hinners
Pindarus....................................Sam Needham
Calpurnia...................................Helen Ross
Portia......................................Mary Darr

Left: Charlton Heston, David Bradley
Top: Grosvenor Glenn, David Bradley
Below: Grosvenor Glenn, Harold Tasker,
Charlton Heston, David Bradley

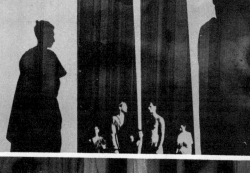

Charlton Heston

Charlton Heston, Grosvenor Glenn

127

Richard Jaeckel, Shirley Booth, Terry Moore
Center: Walter Kelley, Shirley Booth, Terry Moore

Shirley Booth, Burt Lancaster
Center: Shirley Booth, Burt Lancas

Top: Burt Lancaster, Shirley Booth, Richard Jaeckel, Terry Moore

(PARAMOUNT)

COME BACK, LITTLE SHEBA

Producer, Hal B. Wallis; Director, Daniel
; Screenplay by Ketti Frings; Based on
by William Inge; Music by Franz Waxman.

CAST

Delaney	Burt Lancaster
Delaney	Shirley Booth
Buckholder	Terry Moore
Fisher	Richard Jaeckel
nderson	Philip Ober
Goffman	Liza Golm
	Walter Kelley

Shirley Booth, Burt Lancaster
Top and Left: Shirley Booth, Burt Lancaster

Arlene Dahl

David Niven in
"The Lady Says No"

Jimmy Ellison, Lois Hall, Johnny Mack Brown in
"Texas City"

LADY SAYS NO (UNITED ARTISTS) Pro-
rs, Frank Ross and John Stillman, Jr.; Director,
k Ross; Screenplay by Robert Russell. CAST:
Caulfield, David Niven, James Robertson Jus-
Lenore Lonergan, Frances Bavier, Peggy
y, Henry Jones, Jeff York, George Davis, Rob-
Williams, Mary Lawrence.

CAGO CALLING (UNITED ARTISTS) Pro-
r, Peter Berneis; Director, John Reinhardt; As-
te Producer, Kurt Kirsch; Assistant Director,
n Carter. CAST: Dan Duryea, Mary Ander-
Gordon Gebert, Ross Elliott, Melinda Plow-
, Roy Engle, Jean Harvey, Judy Brubaker, Bob
n, Bud Stork, Mark Lowell, Glaze Loman, Mel
e, Marsha Jones, Rudy McKool, Roy Glen,
ren Raker.

THER MAN'S POISON (UNITED ARTISTS)
ucer, Daniel M. Angel; Director, Irving Rap-
Screenplay by Val Guest; Based on Play by
ie Sands; Music by Paul Sawtell; Presented by
glas Fairbanks, Jr. and Daniel M. Angel.
T: Bette Davis, Gary Merrill, Emlyn Williams,
ony Steel, Barbara Murray, Reginald Beckwith,
a Morris.

TEXAS CITY (MONOGRAM) Producer, Vincent M.
Fennelly; Director, Lewis Collins; Assistant Direc-
tor, Melville Shyer; Screenplay by Joseph F. Poland.
CAST: Johnny Mack Brown, Jimmy Ellison, Lois
Hall, Lorna Thayer, Lane Bradford, Marshall J.
Reed, Terry L. Frost, Lyle Talbot, Pierce Lyden,
Lennie Osborne, John Hart, Stanley Price.

SMOKY CANYON (COLUMBIA) Producer, Colbert
Clark; Director, Fred F. Sears; Assistant Director,
Jim Nicholson. CAST: Charles Starrett, Smiley
Burnette, Jack Mahoney, Dani Sue Nolan, Tristram
Coffin, Larry Hudson, Cris Alcaide, Sandy Sanders,
Forrest Taylor, Charles Stevens, Boyd "Red" Mor-
gan, LeRoy Johnson.

WOMAN IN THE DARK (REPUBLIC) Producer,
Herbert J. Yates; Associate Producer, Stephen Auer;
Director, George Blair; Screenplay by Albert
DeMond; Based on Play by Nicholas Cosentino;
Music by Stanley Wilson. CAST: Penny Edwards,
Ross Elliott, Rick Vallin, Richard Benedict, Argen-
tina Brunetti, Martin Garralaga, Edit Angold, Peter
Brocco, Barbara Billingsley, John Doucette, Richard
Irving, Luther Crockett, Carl Thompson, Charles
Sullivan.

yn Williams, Bette Davis, Gary Merrill in
"Another Man's Poison"

Robert Preston, Harold Lang in
"Cloudburst"

POSSESSED (REPUBLIC) Producer, James
a; Associate Producer, Roy Kellino; Directors,
m Spier and Roy Kellino; Screenplay by
a Kellino and James Mason; Based on Novel
mela Kellino; Music by Nathan Scott. CAST:
Mason, June Havoc, Stephen Dunne, Fay
ton, Pamela Kellino, Steven Geray, Diana
s, Odette Myrtil, Eileen Erskine, John P.
han, Enid Mosier, Judy Osborn, Constance
dish, Alma Lawton, Ann Grevler, Tonyna
Dolly, Hazel Franklyn.

CLOUDBURST (UNITED ARTISTS) Producer,
Alexander Paal; Director, Francis Searle; Screen-
play by Francis Searle and Leo Marks; Based on
play by Leo Marks; Music by Frank Spencer;
CAST: Robert Preston, Elizabeth Sellars, Colin
Tapley, Sheila Burrell, Harold Lang, Mary Ger-
maine, Thomas Heathcote, George Woodbridge,
Lyn Evans, Edith Sharpe, James Mills, Daphne
Anderson, Edward Lexy, Noel Howlett, Robert
Brown, Charles Saynor, Gerald Case, Fredric Steger,
Stanley Baker, Martin Boddey.

Roddy McDowall, Kristine Miller, Rand Brooks in
"The Steel Fist"

Clayton Moore, Charles Harvey in
"Buffalo Bill"

THE STEEL FIST (MONOGRAM) Producer-Director, Wesley Barry; Screenplay by C. K. Kivari; Story by Phyllis Parker. CAST: Roddy McDowall, Kristine Miller, Harry Lauter, Rand Brooks, Byron Foulger, Kate Lawson, Murray Alper, Bob Peoples, Gil Perkins, Fred Krone.

NIGHT RAIDERS (MONOGRAM) Producer, Vincent M. Fennelly; Director, Howard Bretherton; Assistant Director, Melville Shyer; Screenplay by Maurice Tombragel. CAST: Whip Wilson, Tom Farrell, Fuzzy Knight, Lois Hall, Steve Clark, Terry Frost, Marshall Reed, Lane Bradford, Iron Eyes Cody, Carol Henry, Ed Cassidy, Forrest Taylor, Stanley Price, Roy Butler.

HAREM GIRL (COLUMBIA) Producer, Wallace MacDonald; Director, Edward Bernds; Assistant Director, Carter DeHaven; Dance Director, Lee Scott; Screenplay by Edward Bernds and Elwood Ullman; Story by Edward Bernds. CAST: Joan Davis, Peggie Castle, Arthur Blake, Paul Marion, Donald Randolph, Henry Brandon, Minerva Urecal, Peter Mamakos, John Dehner, Peter Brocco, Rus Conklin, Wilson Millar, Ric Roman, Nick Thompson, Alan Foster, Robert Tafur, Shepard Menken.

COLORADO SUNDOWN (REPUBLIC) Prod Herbert J. Yates; Associate Producer, Edwar White; Director, William Witney; Screenplay Eric Taylor, William Lively; Story by Eric Ta Music by R. Dale Butts. CAST: Rex Allen, K Mary Ellen Kay, Slim Pickens, June Vincent, Graham, John Daheim, Louise Beavers, Ch Clute, Clarence Straight, The Republic Rh Riders.

ONE BIG AFFAIR (UNITED ARTISTS) Prod Benedict Bogeaus; Director, Peter Godfrey; A tant Director, Ignacio Villarreal; Screenplay Leo Townsend; Adaptation by Francis Swann; by George Bricker; Music by L. Hernandez Br CAST: Evelyn Keyes, Dennis O'Keefe, Mary A son, Connie Gilchrist, Thurston Hall, Gus Schi Jose Torvay, Charles Musqued, Andrew Velaj

BUFFALO BILL (UNITED ARTISTS) Produ Edward Finney, B. B. Ray; Director, B. B. Story and Screenplay by Sam Neuman and Tanchuck; Music by Frank Sanucci. CAST: ton Moore, Slim Andrews, Rod Redwing, Yowlachie, Chief Thundercloud, Charles Ha Shooting Star, Sharon Dexter, Eddie Phillips, Hubbard, Helena Dare, Charles Harvey.

John Dehner, Joan Davis, Paul Marion,
Peter Brocco in
"Harem Girl"

David Wolfe, Beverly Tyler, Leif Ericks
Audie Murphy in
"The Cimarron Kid

INDIAN UPRISING (COLUMBIA) Producer, Bernard Small; Director, Ray Nazarro; Assistant Directors, Gilbert Kay, Milton Feldman; Screenplay by Kenneth Gamet, Richard Schayer; Story by Richard Schayer. CAST: George Montgomery, Audrey Long, Carl Benton Reid, Eugene Iglesias, John Baer, Joe Sawyer, Robert Dover, Eddy Waller, Douglas Kennedy, Robert Shayne, Miguel Inclan, Hugh Sanders, John Call, Robert Griffin, Hank Patterson, Fay Roope, Peter Thompson.

THE CIMARRON KID (UNIVERSAL) Prod Ted Richmond; Director, Budd Boetticher; Sc play by Louis Stevens; Story by Louis Stevens Kay Lenard; Color by Technicolor. CAST: A Murphy, Beverly Tyler, James Best, Yvette D John Hudson, Leif Erickson, Noah Beery, Hubbard, Hugh O'Brian, Palmer Lee, Rand B William Reynolds, Roy Roberts, David Wolfe, Bromfield, Frank Silvera, Richard Garland, E Baxter.

rge Macready, Geraldine Brooks, Glenn Ford
in "The Green Glove"

THE OLD WEST (COLUMBIA) Producer, Armand Schaefer; Director, George Archainbaud; Assistant Director, Paul Donnelly; Screenplay by Gerald Geraghty; A Gene Autry Production. CAST: Gene Autry, Pat Buttram, Gail Davis, Lyle Talbot, Louis Jean Heydt, House Peters, Sr., House Peters, Jr., Dick Jones, Kathy Johnson, Don Harvey, Dee Pollock, Raymond L. Morgan, James Craven, Tom London, Frank Marvin.

THE GREEN GLOVE (UNITED ARTISTS) Producer, Georges Maurer; Director, Rudolph Mate; Story and Screenplay by Charles Bennett; Music by Joseph Kosma; Associate Producer, Detmar Walter; Assistant Director, Gilbert Mandelik. CAST: Glenn Ford, Geraldine Brooks, Cedric Hardwicke, George Macready, Gaby Andre, Jany Holt, Roger Treville, Georges Tabet, Meg Lemonnier, Paul Bonifas, Juliette Greco, Jean Bretonniers.

WACO (MONOGRAM) Producer, Vincent M. Fennelly; Director, Lewis Collins; Assistant Director, Melville Shyer; Screenplay by Dan Ullman, Music by Raoul Kraushaar; A Silvermine Production. CAST: Wild Bill Elliott, Stanford Jolley, Pamela Blake, Paul Fierra, Rand Brooks, Rory Mallinson, Pierce Lyden, Terry Frost, Lane Bradford, Richard Avonde, Ray Bennett, Richard Paxton.

FORT OSAGE (MONOGRAM) Producer, Walter Mirisch; Director, Lesley Selander; Assistant Director, Edward Morey, Jr.; Screenplay by Dan Ullman. CAST: Rod Cameron, Jane Nigh, Morris Ankrum, Douglas Kennedy, John Ridgely, William Phipps, Stanford Jolley, Dorothy Adams, Ann Kimbell, Hal Baylor, Myron Healey, Lane Bradford, Russ Conway, Barbara Allen.

THE HAWK OF WILD RIVER (COLUMBIA) Producer, Colbert Clark; Director, Fred F. Sears; Assistant Director, Paul Donnelly; Screenplay by Howard J. Green. CAST: Charles Starrett, Smiley Burnette, Jack Mahoney, Clayton Moore, Edwin Parker, Jim Diehl, Lane Chandler, Syd Saylor, John Cason, LeRoy Johnson, Jack Carry, Sam Flint, Donna Hall.

THE FIRST TIME (COLUMBIA) Producer, Harold Hecht; Director, Frank Tashlin; Assistant Director, Carter DeHaven; Music by Frederick Hollander; Screenplay by Jean Rouverol, Hugo Butler, Frank Tashlin, Dane Lussier; Based on Story by Jean Rouverol, Hugo Butler; A Norma Production. CAST: Robert Cummings, Barbara Hale, Bill Goodwin, Jeff Donnell, Carl Benton Reid, Mona Barrie, Kathleen Comegys, Paul Harvey, Cora Witherspoon, Bea Benaderet.

Tom Ewell, Julia Adams in
"Finders Keepers"

Karin Himbold, Bonar Colleano in
"A Tale of Five Women"

FINDERS KEEPERS (UNIVERSAL) Producer, Leonard Goldstein; Director, Frederick de Cordova; Story and Screenplay by Richard Morris; Music by Hans J. Salter. CAST: Tom Ewell, Julia Adams, Evelyn Varden, "Dusty" Henley, Harvey Lembeck, Harold Vermilyea.

FLAME OF ARABY (UNIVERSAL) Producer, Leonard Goldstein; Director, Charles Lamont; Story and Screenplay by Gerald Drayson Adams; Dance Director, Harold Belfer; Associate Producer, Ross Hunter, Color by Technicolor. CAST: Maureen O'Hara, Jeff Chandler, Maxwell Reed, Susan Cabot, Lon Chaney, Buddy Baer, Richard Egan, Royal Ano, Neville Brand, Henry Brandon.

A TALE OF FIVE WOMEN (UNITED ARTISTS) Producer, Alexander Paal; Directors, Romollo Marcellini, Geza von Cziffra, Wolfgang Staudte, E. E. Reinert, Montgomery Tully; Screenplay by Richard Llewellyn, Piero Tellini, Guenter Weisenborn, Jacques Companeez, Patrick Kirwin; Music by Hans May, Joseph Hajos. CAST: Bonar Colleano, Barbara Kelly, Anne Vernon, Karin Himbold, Lily Kahn, Danny Green, Carl Jaffe, MacDonald Park, Aletha Orr, Lana Morris, Eva Bartok, Gina Lollobrigida, Geoffrey Sumner, Philip Leaver, Annette Poivre, Charles Irwin, Arthur Gomez, Andrew Irvine, Dany Dauberson.

133

Here Come the Nelsons

Allan "Rocky" Lane and Black Jack in "Leadville Gunslinger"

HERE COME THE NELSONS (UNIVERSAL) Producer, Aaron Rosenberg; Director, Frederick de Cordova; Story and Screenplay by Ozzie Nelson, Donald Nelson, William Davenport; Based on Radio Show. CAST: Ozzie Nelson, Harriet Nelson, David Nelson, Ricky Nelson, Rock Hudson, Barbara Lawrence, Ann Doran, Jim Backus, Gale Gordon, Paul Harvey, Ed Max, Sheldon Leonard, Chubby Johnson.

LEADVILLE GUNSLINGER (REPUBLIC) Producer, Herbert J. Yates; Associate Producer-Director, Harry Keller; Screenplay by M. Coates Webster; Music by Stanley Wilson. CAST: Allan "Rocky" Lane, Black Jack, Eddy Waller, Grant Withers, Elaine Riley, Roy Barcroft, Richard Crane, Stanford Jolley, Kenneth MacDonald, Mickey Simpson, Ed Hinton, Art Dillard, Wesley Hudman.

THE LAST MUSKETEER (REPUBLIC) Producer, Herbert J. Yates; Associate Producer, Edward J. White; Director, William Witney; Screenplay by Arthur E. Orloff; Music by Nathan Scott. CAST: Rex Allen, Koko, Mary Ellen Kay, Slim Pickens, James Anderson, Boyd "Red" Morgan, Monte Montague, Michael Hall, Alan Bridge, Stan Jones, The Republic Rhythm Riders.

FOR MEN ONLY (LIPPERT) Producer-Director, Paul Henreid; Screenplay by Lou Morheim; Story by Lou Morheim and Herbert Margolies; Music by Laving Friedman; An N-H Production. CAST: Paul Henreid, Robert Sherman, Russell Johnson, Margaret Field, Kathleen Hughes, Vera Miles, James Dobson, Douglas Kennedy, Robert Carson, Virgin Mullen, Steven Clark, Chris Drake, Bob Chapman, O. Z. Whitehead, Arthur Marshall, Fran Mathias.

MAN BAIT (LIPPERT) Producer, Anthony Hind; Director, Terence Fisher; Screenplay by Frederic Knott; Story by James Hadley Chase. CAST: George Brent, Marguerite Chapman, Diana Dors, Raymond Huntley, Peter Reynolds, Isabel Dean, Conrad Philips.

JUNGLE JIM IN THE FORBIDDEN LAND (COLUMBIA) Producer, Sam Katzman; Director, Lew Landers; Screenplay by Samuel Newman; Based on newspaper feature; Assistant Director, Jack Corrick. CAST: Johnny Weissmuller, Angela Greene, Jean Willes, Lester Matthews, William Tannen, George Eldredge, Frederic Berest, Clem Erickson, Irmgard Helen H. Raschke, William Fawcett, Fran Jacquet.

Judy Canova in "Oklahoma Annie"

John Bromfield, Leo Gorcey, Paul Bryar in "Hold That Line"

OKLAHOMA ANNIE (REPUBLIC) Producer, Herbert J. Yates; Associate Producer, Sidney Picker; Director, R. G. Springsteen; Screenplay by Jack Townley; Story by Jack Townley and Charles E. Roberts; Music by Nathan Scott; Trucolor by Consolidated. CAST: Judy Canova, John Russell, Grant Withers, Roy Barcroft, Emmett "Pappy" Lynn, Frank Ferguson, Minerva Urecal, Houseley Stevenson, Almira Sessions, Allen Jenkins, Maxine Gates, Emory Parnell, Denver Pyle, House Peters, Jr., Andrew Tombes, Fuzzy Knight, Si Jenks.

HOLD THAT LINE (MONOGRAM) Producer, Jerry Thomas; Director, William Beaudine; Assistant Director, Edward Morey, Jr.; Screenplay by Charles Marion and Tim Ryan. CAST: Leo Gorcey, Huntz Hall, Gil Stratton, Jr., David Gorcey, Bennie Bartlett, Bernard Gorcey, Taylor Holmes, Francis Pierlot, Pierre Watkin, John Bromfield, Bob Nichols, Mona Knox, Gloria Winters, Veda Ann Borg, Al Eben.

NAVAJO (LIPPERT) Producer, Hall Bartlett; Written and Directed by Norman Foster; Music by Leith Stevens. CAST: Francis Kee Telle, John Mitchell, Billy Draper, Mrs. Teller, Sammy Ogg.

Zachary Scott, Veronica Lake in
"Stronghold"

Jane Nigh, John Archer in
"Rodeo"

RONGHOLD (LIPPERT) Producer, Olallo Ru-
, Jr.; Director, Steve Sekely; Assistant Director,
s Abadi; Screenplay by Wells Root. CAST:
onica Lake, Zachary Scott, Arturo de Cordova,
a Lacedo, Alfonso Bedoya, Yadiro Jiminez, Fan-
Schiller, Gilberto Gonzales, Carlos Muzquiz,
derick A. Mack, Roc Galbin, Gustavo Rojo,
ie Ajay, Felipe de Alba.

E MAN FROM BLACK HILLS (MONOGRAM)
ducer, Vincent M. Fennelly; Director, Thomas
r; Assistant Director, Melville Shyer; Screen-
oaud by Joseph O'Donnell. CAST: Johnny Mack
wn, James Ellison, Randy Brooks, Lane Brad-
l, Stanford Jolley, Robert Bray, Stanley Price,
aver Pyle, Ray Bennett, Joel Allen, Stanley
drews, Florence Lake.

HT STAGE TO GALVESTON (COLUMBIA)
ducer, Armand Schaefer; Director, George Arch-
baud; Assistant Director, Paul Donnelly; Screen-
y by Norman S. Hall. CAST: Gene Autry,
mpion, Pat Buttram, Virginia Huston, Thurs-
Hall, Judy Nugent, Robert Livingston, Harry
ding, Robert Bice, Frank Sully, Clayton Moore,
nk Rawls, Steve Clark, Harry Lauter, Robert
ton, Lois Austin.

RODEO (MONOGRAM) Producer, Walter Mirisch;
Assistant Producer, Richard Heermance; Director,
William Beaudine; Assistant Director, Edward Mo-
rey, Jr.; Screenplay by Charles R. Marion; Color by
Cinecolor. CAST: Jane Nigh, John Archer, Wal-
lace Ford, Gary Gray, Frances Rafferty, Jim Ban-
non, Sarah Hayden, Frank Ferguson, Myron Healey,
Ann Doran, Fuzzy Knight, Dave Willock, Milton
Kibbee.

STRANGE WORLD (UNITED ARTISTS) Producer,
O. A. Bayer, Franz Eichhorn; Story and Screenplay
by Al O'Camp, F. E. Eichhorn, O. A. Bayer; Music
by W. Schultz-Porto Alegro and Emil Velazco.
CAST: Angelica Hauff, Alexander Carlos, America
Cabral, Carmen Brown, Kumatzaikuma, Ary Jartul,
Griyo Sobrinho, W. Hardt.

THE TREASURE OF LOST CANYON (UNIVER-
SAL) Producer, Leonard Goldstein; Director, Ted
Tetzlaff; Screenplay by Brainerd Duffield and Em-
erson Crocker; Based on Story by Robert Louis
Stevenson; Color by Technicolor. CAST: William
Powell, Julia Adams, Charles Drake, Henry Hull,
Rosemary De Camp, Tommy Ivo, Chubby Johnson,
John Doucette, Marvin Press, Frank Wilcox.

c Knowles, Angela Lansbury, Mark Stevens in
"Mutiny"

Alexander Carlos, Angelica Hauff in
"Strange World"

TINY (UNITED ARTISTS) Producers, Maurice
Frank King; Director, Edward Dmytryk;
enplay by Philip Yordan and Sidney Harmon;
d on Story by Hollister Noble; Music by Dimi-
iomkin; Color by Technicolor. CAST: Mark
ens, Angela Lansbury, Patric Knowles, Gene
is, Rhys Williams, Robert Osterloh, Peter Broc-
Norman Leavitt, Gene Roth, Walter Sande,
ton Moore, Morris Ankrum, Todd Karnes, Louis
Heydt, Robin Hughes, Crane Whitley, Emer-
Treacy, Harry Antrim.

SCANDAL SHEET (COLUMBIA) Producer, Ed-
ward Small; Director, Phil Karlson; Assistant Di-
rector, Fredrick Briskin; Screenplay by Ted Sher-
deman, Eugene Ling, James Poe; Based on Novel
by Samuel Fuller; Music by George Duning. CAST:
John Derek, Donna Reed, Broderick Crawford,
Rosemary De Camp, Henry O'Neil, Henry Morgan,
James Millican, Griff Barnett, Jonathan Hale, Pierre
Watkin, Ida Moore, Ralph Reed, Luther Crockett,
Charles Cane, Jay Adler, Don Beddoe.

Nelson Leigh, Lon Chaney, Paul Henreid, Robert Clary in "Thief of Damascus"

Slim Pickens, Rex Allen in "Border Saddle Mates"

WINGS OF DANGER (LIPPERT) Producer, Anthony Hinds; Director, Terence Fisher; Assistant Director, James Sangster; Screenplay by John Gilling; Story by Elleston Trevor and Packham Webb. CAST: Zachary Scott, Robert Beatty, Kay Kendall, Naomi Chance, Arthur Lane, Colin Tapley, Diane Cilento, Harold Lang, Jack Allen, Sheila Raynor, Courtney Hope, June Ashley, Natasha Sokolova, June Mitchell, James Steel, Russ Allen, Darcy Conyers.

THIEF OF DAMASCUS (COLUMBIA) Producer, Sam Katzman; Director, Will Jason; Assistant Director, Carl Hiecke; Screenplay by Robert E. Kent; Color by Technicolor. CAST: Paul Henreid, John Sutton, Jeff Donnell, Lon Chaney, Elena Verdugo, Helen Gilbert, Robert Clary, Edward Colmans, Nelson Leigh, Philip Van Zandt, Leonard Penn, Larry Stewart, Robert Conte.

THE GUNMAN (MONOGRAM) Producer, Vincent M. Fennelly; Director, Lewis Collins; Assistant Director, Melville Shyer; Screenplay by Fred Myton. CAST: Whip Wilson, Fuzzy Knight, Rand Brooks, Terry Frost, Stanford Jolley, Phyllis Coates, Lane Bradford, Gregg Barton, Russ Whiteman, Richard Avonde, Bob Bray.

BORDER SADDLEMATES (REPUBLIC) Produ Herbert J. Yates; Associate Producer, Edwarc White; Director, William Witney; Music by S ley Wilson; Screenplay by Albert DeMond. CA Rex Allen, Koko, Mary Ellen Kay, Slim Pick Roy Barcroft, Forrest Taylor, Jimmie Moss, Murray, Keith McConnell, Mark Hanna, Repu Rhythm Riders.

THE LION AND THE HORSE (WARNER BR Producer, Bryan Foy; Director, Louis King; A tant Director, William Kissel; Screenplay by C Wilbur; Music by Max Steiner; Color by War color. CAST: Steve Cochran, Wildfire, Ray T Bob Steele, Harry Antrim, George O'Hanlon, Sh Jackson, Ed Hinton, William Fawcett, House Pe Jr., Lee Roberts, Lane Chandler, Charles Stev Jack Williams, Tom Tyler, Billy Dix, Steve Pec

ROSE OF CIMARRON (20th CENTURY-F Producer, Edward L. Alperson; Director, H Keller; Screenplay by Maurice Geraghty; Colo Natural Cblor. CAST: Jack Buetel, Mala Pow Bill Williams, Jim Davis, Dick Curtis, Lane B ford, William Phipps, Bob Steele, Alex Gerry, lian Bronson, Art Smith, Monte Blue, Argen Brunetti.

Jack Williams, Steve Cochran, Bob Steele, Lane Chandler in "The Lion And The Horse"

Mala Powers, Jack Buetel in "Rose of Cimarron"

VALLEY OF THE EAGLES (LIPPERT) Producer, Nat Bronsten; Associate Producer, George Willoughby; Director, Terence Young; Assistant Director, Basil Keys; Screenplay by Terence Young; Music by Nino Rota. CAST: Jack Warner, Nadia Gray, John McCallum, Anthony Dawson, Mary Laura Wood, Norman MacOwan, Alfred Maurstad, Martin Boddey, Christopher Lee, Ewen Solon, Niama Wiwstrand, Peter Blitz, Sahar Crawford, Molly Warner, Triliot Billquist, Gosta Cederlund, Sten Lindgren, Kurt Sundstrom, Holger Kax.

BLACK HILLS AMBUSH (REPUBLIC) Prod Herbert J. Yates; Associate Producer-Dire Harry Keller; Screenplay by Ronald Davidson M. Coates Webster; Music by Stanley W CAST: Allan "Rocky" Lane, Eddy Waller, L Banning, Roy Barcroft, Michael Hall, John Vc Edward Cassidy, John Cason, Wesley Hud Michael Barton, Black Jack.

WILD STALLION (MONOGRAM) Produce ter Mirisch; Director, Lewis Collins; Screenpla Dan Ullman; Color by Cinecolor. CAST: Johnson, Edgar Buchanan, Hayden Rorke, Lindgren, Martha Hyer, Hugh Beaumont, Don gerty, John Halloran, Barbara Woodell, Sta Jolley, Don Garner.

Claire Trevor, John Russell in
"Hoodlum Empire"

Stanley Clements, Elena Verdugo in
"Jet Job"

HOODLUM EMPIRE (REPUBLIC) Producer, Herbert J. Yates; Associate Producer-Director, Joseph Kane; Screenplay by Bruce Manning and Bob Considine; Story by Bob Considine; Music by Nathan Scott. CAST: Brian Donlevy, Claire Trevor, Forrest Tucker, Vera Ralston, Luther Adler, John Russell, Gene Lockhart, Grant Withers, Taylor Holmes, Roy Barcroft, William Murphy, Richard Jaeckel, Don Beddoe, Roy Roberts, Richard Benedict, Philip Van, Damian O'Flynn, Pat Flaherty.

THE FABULOUS SENORITA (REPUBLIC) Producer, Herbert J. Yates; Associate Producer, Sidney Picker; Director, R. G. Springsteen; Screenplay by Charles E. Roberts and Jack Townley; Story by Charles R. Marion and Jack Townley; Music by Stanley Wilson; Dance Director, Antonio Triani. CAST: Estelita, Robert Clarke, Nestor Paiva, Marin Kaplan, Rita Moreno, Leon Belasco, Tito Renaldo, Tom Powers, Emory Parnell, Olin Howlin, Tito Scotti, Martin Garralaga.

JET JOB (MONOGRAM) Producer, Ben Schwalb; Director, William Beaudine; Screenplay by Charles Marion. CAST: Stanley Clements, Elena Verdugo, John Litel, Bob Nichols, Tom Powers, Todd Karns, Russ Conway, Steve Roberts, John Kellogg, Bob Peoples, William Forrest, William Tannen.

APACHE COUNTRY (COLUMBIA) Producer, Armand Schaefer; Director, George Archainbaud; Screenplay by Norman S. Hall. CAST: Gene Autry, Pat Buttram, Carolina Cotton, Harry Lauter, Mary Scott, Sydney Mason, Francis X. Bushman, Gregg Barton, Tom London, Byron Foulger, Frank Matts, Mickey Simpson, Cass County Boys, Tony Whitecloud's Jemez Indians.

DESERT PURSUIT (MONOGRAM) Producer, Lindsley Parson; Director, George Blair; Screenplay by W. Scott Darling; Based on Story by Kenneth Perkins. CAST: Wayne Morris, Virginia Grey, Anthony Caruso, George Tobias, John Doucette, Emmett Lynn, Bill Wilkerson, Bob Rice, Gloria Talbot, Frank Lackteen.

WILD HORSE AMBUSH (REPUBLIC) Producer, Herbert J. Yates, Associate Producer, Rudy Ralston; Director, Fred C. Brannon, Screenplay by William Lively; Music by Stanley Wilson. CAST: Michael Chapin, Eilene Janssen, James Bell, Richard Avonde, Roy Barcroft, Julian Rivero, Movita, Drake Smith, Scott Lee, Alex Montoya, John Daheim, Ted Cooper, Wayne Burson.

Joyce Holden, Scott Brady, John Lund in
"Bronco Buster"

John Forsythe, Joan Camden in
"The Captive City"

LARAMIE MOUNTAINS (COLUMBIA) Producer, Albert Clark; Director, Ray Nazarro; Assistant Director, Jack Corrick; Screenplay by Barry Shipman. CAST: Charles Starrett, Smiley Burnette, Jack Mahoney, Fred Sears, Marshall Reed, Rory Mallinson, Zon Murray, John War Eagle, Bob Wilke.

BRONCO BUSTER (UNIVERSAL) Producer, Ted Richmond; Director, Budd Boetticher; Screenplay by Horace McCoy and Lillie Hayward; Based on Story by Peter B. Kyne; Color by Technicolor. CAST: John Lund, Scott Brady, Joyce Holden, Chill Wills, Don Haggerty, Dan Poore, Bill Williams, Casey Tibbs, Pete Crump, Manuel Enos.

THE CAPTIVE CITY (UNITED ARTISTS) Producer, Theron Warth; Director, Robert Wise; Screenplay by Karl Kamb and Alvin Josephy, Jr.; Based on Story by Alvin Josephy, Jr.; Music by Jerome Moross. CAST: Senator Estes Kefauver, John Forsythe, Joan Camden, Harold J. Kennedy, Marjorie Crossland, Victor Sutherland, Ray Teal, Martin Milner, Geraldine Hall, Hal K. Dawson, Ian Wolfe, Gladys Hurlbut, Jess Kirkpatrick, Paul Newlan, Frances Morris, Paul Brinegar, Patricia Goldwater, Robert Gorrell, Glenn Judd, William C. Miller.

137

John Archer, Douglas Dick in "A Yank In Indo-China"

John Archer, Helen Ford, Mickey Rooney, Anne James in "Sound Off"

LOAN SHARK (LIPPERT) Producer, Bernard Luber; Director, Seymour Friedman; Screenplay by Martin Rackin and Eugene Ling; Story by Martin Rackin. CAST: George Raft, Dorothy Hart, Paul Stewart, Helen Westcott, John Hoyt, Henry Slate, William Phipps, Russell Johnson, Benny Baker, Margia Dean, Larry Dobkin.

KANSAS TERRITORY (MONOGRAM) Producer, Vincent M. Fennelly; Director, Lewis Collins; Screenplay by Dan Ullman. CAST: Wild Bill Elliott, Peggy Stewart, Lane Bradford, Marshall Reed, Stanford Jolley, House Peters, Jr., Lyle Talbot, Terry Frost, John Hart, William Fawcett.

RETURN OF GILBERT AND SULLIVAN (LIPPERT) Producer, Irving Allen, Dance Director, Val Raset; Screenplay by Sid Kuller. CAST: Melville Cooper, Tudor Owen, Billy Gray, Mara Lynn, Pat Hogan, Joe Graves, Scatman Crothers, Marie Bryant, Dick Carlin, Al Hammer, The Sportsmen, Dee Turnell.

A YANK IN INDO-CHINA (COLUMBIA) Producer, Sam Katzman; Director, Wallace A. Grissell; Screenplay by Samuel Newman. CAST: John Archer, Douglas Dick, Jean Willes, Maura Murphy, Hayward Soo Hoo, Don Harvey, Harold Fong, Rory Mallinson, Leonard Penn, Kamtong, Pierre Watkin, Peter Chang.

WITHOUT WARNING (UNITED ARTISTS) Producers, Arthur Gardner and Jules Levy; Director, Arnold Laven; Story and Screenplay by Bill Raynor; Music by Herschel Burke Gilbert. CAST: Adam Williams, Meg Randall, Edward Binns, Harlan Warde, John Maxwell, Angela Stevens, Byron Kane, Charles Tannen, Marilee Phelps, Robert Foulk, Connie Vera, Robert Shayne.

RED BALL EXPRESS (UNIVERSAL) Producer, Aaron Rosenberg; Director, Budd Boetticher; Screenplay by John Michael Hayes; Story by Marc Klauber and Billy Grady, Jr. CAST: Jeff Chandler, Alex Nicol, Charles Drake, Hugh O'Brian, Frank Chase, Jack Kelly, Judith Braun, Cindy Garner, Jacqueline Deval, Howard Petrie, Richard Garland, Palmer Lee, Sidney Poitier, Bubber Johnson, Jack Warden, Robert Davis.

SOUND OFF (COLUMBIA) Producer, Jonie Taps, Director, Richard Quine; Screenplay by Blake Edwards and Richard Quine; Dances Staged by White; Music by George Duning; Color by SuperecineColor. CAST: Mickey Rooney, Anne James, Sammy White, John Archer, Gordon Jones, Wally Cassell, Arthur Space, Pat Williams, Marshall Reed, Helen Ford, Mary Lou Geer, Boyd "Red" Morgan.

Cyril Cusack, Jennifer Jones in "The Wild Heart"

Laurette Luez, Johnny Sheffield in "African Treasure"

AFRICAN TREASURE (MONOGRAM) Producer, Walter Mirisch; Director, Ford Beebe; Story and Screenplay by Ford Beebe. CAST: Johnny Sheffield, Laurette Luez, Leonard Mudie, Arthur Space, Lane Bradford, Martin Garralaga, Lyle Talbot, Robert Whitfield, James Adamson, Jack Williams.

GOBS AND GALS (REPUBLIC) Producer, Herbert J. Yates; Associate Producer, Sidney Picker; Director, R. G. Springsteen; Screenplay by Arthur T. Horman; Music by Stanley Wilson. CAST: George and Bert Bernard, Robert Hutton, Cathy Downs, Gordon Jones, Florence Marly, Leon Belasco, Emory Parnell, Leonid Kinskey, Tommy Rettig, Minerva Urecal, Olin Howlin, Donald MacBride, Henry Kulky.

THE WILD HEART (RKO) Written, Directed and Produced by Michael Powell and Emeric Pressburger; Adapted from Novel by Mary Webb; Music by Brian Easdale; Color by Technicolor; A Selznick Picture. CAST: Jennifer Jones, David Farrar, Cyril Cusack, Esmond Knight, Sybil Thorndike, Hugh Griffith, Edward Chapman, Beatrice Varley, George Cole, Frances Clare, Valentine Dunn, Richmond Nairne, Owen Holder, Raymond Rollett, Bartlett Millins, Arthur Reynolds, Gerald Lawson, A. Tetheradge, Peter Dunlop, Gerald Lawson, Lo Philips.

ert Berghof, Peter Graves, Andrea King in
"Red Planet Mars"

Jon Hall, Christine Larson, Harry Cording in
"Brave Warrior"

PLANET MARS (UNITED ARTISTS) Pro-
, Anthony Veiller; Director, Harry Horner;
nplay by John L. Balderston and Anthony
r; Based on Play by John L. Balderston and
Hoare; Music by Mahlon Merrick. CAST:
Graves, Andrea King, Orley Lindgren, Bay-
Veiller, Walter Sande, Marvin Miller, Herbert
of, Willis Bouchey, Richard Powers, Morris
m, Lewis Martin, House Peters, Jr., Claude
in, Gene Roth, John Topa, Bill Kennedy,
Leonard, Vince Barnett.

NARROW MARGIN (RKO) Producer, Stan-
ubin; Director, Richard Fleischer; Screenplay
rl Felton; Story by Martin Goldsmith and Jack
ard. CAST: Charles McGraw, Marie Windsor,
eline White, Queenie Leonard, David Clarke,
Virgo, Don Beddoe, Paul Maxey, Harry Her-
Gordon Gebert.

TABARIN (REPUBLIC) Producer, Herbert J.
; Associate Producer, Herman Millakowsky;
tor, Philip Ford; Screenplay by Houston
h; Music by R. Dale Butts. CAST: Muriel
ence, William Ching, Claire Carleton, Steve
e, Steven Geray, Carl Milletaire, Jan Rubini,
Powers, Gregory Gay, Adrienne d'Ambricourt,
ert Deans.

BRAVE WARRIOR (COLUMBIA) Producer, Sam
Katzman; Director, Spencer B. Bennet; Screenplay
by Robert E. Kent; Color by Technicolor. CAST:
Jon Hall, Christine Larson, Jay Silverheels, Michael
Ansara, Harry Cording, James Seay, George Eldredge, Leslie Denison, Rory Mallinson, Rusty Wes-
coatt, Bert Davidson, William P. Wilkerson, Gilbert V. Perkins.

CONFIDENCE GIRL (UNITED ARTISTS) Pro-
ducer, Director and Screenplay by Andrew L.
Stone. CAST: Tom Conway, Hillary Brooke, Ed-
die Marr, Dan Riss, Jack Kruschen, John Gallaudet,
Paul Livermore, Aline Towne, Hellen Van Tuyl,
Walter Kingsford, Charlie Collins, Bruce Edwards,
Tyler McVey, Paul Guilfoyle, Edmund Cobb, Pam-
ela Duncan, Barbara Woodell, Madge Crane, Roy
Engel.

GOLD FEVER (MONOGRAM) Producer, John
Calvert; Director, Leslie Goodwins; Music by John-
ny Richards; Screenplay by Edgar C. Anderson, Jr.,
and Cliff Lancaster; Story by John Calvert. CAST:
John Calvert, Ralph Morgan, Ann Cornell, Gene
Roth, Tom Kennedy, Judd Holdren, Danny Rense,
Bobby Graham.

Lund, Harvey Lembeck, Ann Sheridan in
"Just Across The Street"

Ronald Reagan, Doris Day, Gordon Jones in
"The Winning Team"

ACROSS THE STREET (UNIVERSAL) Pro-
, Leonard Goldstein; Director, Joseph Pevney;
nplay by Roswell Rogers and Joel Malone.
: Ann Sheridan, John Lund, Robert Keith,
Kellaway, Harvey Lembeck, Natalie Schafer,
Mowbray, George Eldredge, Burt Mustin,
Bird, Jack Kruchen.

LAW WOMEN (LIPPERT) Producer, Ron
nd; Director, Samuel Newfield; Screenplay by
le Hampton; Color by Cinecolor. CAST:
Windsor, Richard Rober, Alan Nixon, Carla
da, Jacqueline Fontaine, Jackie Coogan, Maria
Billy House, Richard Avonde, Leonard Penn,
Talbot, Brad Johnson.

THE WINNING TEAM (WARNER BROS.) Pro-
ducer, Bryan Foy; Director, Lewis Seiler; Screen-
play by Ted Sherdeman, Seeleg Lester and Mer-
win Gerard; Story by Seeleg Lester and Merwin
Gerard; Music by David Buttolph. CAST: Doris
Day, Ronald Reagan, Frank Lovejoy, Eve Miller,
James Millican, Rusty Tamblyn, Gordon Jones,
Hugh Sanders, Frank Ferguson, Walter Baldwin,
Dorothy Adams, Bonnie Kay Eddie, James Dodd,
Fred Millican, Pat Flaherty, Tom Greenway, Frank
MacFarland, Arthur Page, Tom Browne Henry,
Larry Blake, Frank Marlowe, Kenneth Patterson.

Bill Shirley, Eileen Christy in
"I Dream Of Jeanie"

Preston Foster, Ruth Warren, Lon McAllis
"Montana Territory"

STOLEN FACE (LIPPERT) Producer, Anthony Hinds; Director, Terence Fisher; Screenplay by Richard Landau and Martin Berkeley. CAST: Paul Henreid, Lizabeth Scott, Andre Morell, Mary MacKenzie, John Wood, Susan Stephen, Arnold Ridley, Everley Gregg, Cyril Smith, Janey Burnell, Grace Gavin, Terence O'Reagan, Diana Beaumont, Alexis France, John Bull, Richard Wattis.

I DREAM OF JEANIE (REPUBLIC) Producer, Herbert J. Yates; Director, Allan Dwan; Screenplay by Alan LeMay; Trucolor by Consolidated; Music Adapted by Robert Armbruster. CAST: Ray Middleton, Bill Shirley, Muriel Lawrence, Eileen Christy, Lynn Bari, Richard Simmons, Robert Neil, Andrew Tombes, James Dobson, Percy Helton, Glenn Turnbull, Louise Beavers, James Kirkwood, Carl Dean Switzer, Freddie Moultrie, Rex Allen.

THE ROUGH, TOUGH WEST (COLUMBIA) Producer, Colbert Clark, Director, Ray Nazarro; Screenplay by Barry Shipman. CAST: Charles Starrett, Smiley Burnette, Jack Mahoney, Carolina Cotton, Marshall Reed, Fred Sears, Bert Arnold, Tommy Ivo, Valeria Fisher, Pee Wee King and His Band, Boyd "Red" Morgan.

MONTANA TERRITORY (COLUMBIA) Prod Colbert Clark; Director, Ray Nazarro; Scree by Barry Shipman; Color by Technicolor. C Lon McCallister, Wanda Hendrix, Preston F Hugh Sanders, Jack Flam, Clayton Moore, R Griffin, Myron Healey, Eddy Waller, George sell, Ethan Laidlaw, Frank Matts, Ruth Wa Trevor Bardette, George Chesebro.

WOMAN OF THE NORTH COUNTRY (RE LIC) Producer, Herbert J. Yates; Associate ducer-Director, Joseph Kane; Screenplay by man Reilly Raine; Story by Charles Marquis ren and Prescott Chaplin; Music by R. Dale I Trucolor by Consolidated. CAST: Ruth H Rod Cameron, John Agar, Gale Storm, J. C Naish, Jim Davis, Jay C. Flippen, Taylor Ho Barry Kelley, Grant Withers, Stephen Bel Howard Petrie, Hank Worden, Virginia Briss

JUNCTION CITY (COLUMBIA) Producer, bert Clark; Director, Ray Nazarro; Screenpla Barry Shipman. CAST: Charles Starrett, S Burnette, Jack Mahoney, Kathleen Case, Dehner, Steve Darrell, George Chesebro, Anita tle, Mary Newton, Robert Bice, Hal Price, Taliaferro, Cris Alcaide, Bob Woodward.

Carl Benton Reid, Anthony Dexter, Ron Randell in
"The Brigand"

Lucille Norman, Richard Webb, Randolph :
"Carson City"

THE BRIGAND (COLUMBIA) Director, Phil Karlson; Screenplay by Jesse Lasky, Jr.; Story by George Bruce; Inspired by Alexandre Dumas' Story; Music by Mario Castlenuovo-Tedesco; Choreographer, Eugene Loring; Color by Technicolor; Assistant Director, Carter DeHaven. CAST: Anthony Dexter, Jody Lawrance, Gale Robbins, Anthony Quinn, Carl Benton Reid, Ron Randell, Fay Roope, Carleton Young, Ian MacDonald, Lester Matthews, Barbara Brown, Walter Kingsford, Donald Randolph, Mari Blanchard, Holmes Herbert.

CARSON CITY (WARNER BROS.) Producer vid Weisbart; Director, Andre De Toth; Scree by Sloan Nibley and Winston Miller; Stor Sloan Nibley; Music by David Buttolph; Col Warnercolor. CAST: Randolph Scott, Lucille man, Raymond Massey, Richard Webb, James lican, Larry Keating, George Cleveland, W Haade, Thurston Hall, Vince Barnett.

TELL IT TO THE MARINES (MONOGRAM ducer, Jerry Thomas; Director, William Beau Screenplay by Tim Ryan and Jack Cru CAST: Leo Gorcey, Huntz Hall, David Co Bennie Bartlett, Gil Stratton, Bernard Gorcey, ley Stafford, Murray Alper, Arthur Space, Dell, Paul Maxey, Tim Ryan.

George Montgomery, Karin Booth in
"Cripple Creek"

Ann Blyth, Palmer Lee in
"Sally and Saint Anne"

ONS WEST (MONOGRAM) Producer, Vin-
M. Fennelly; Director, Ford Beebe; Screen-
by Dan Ullman. CAST: Rod Cameron, Peggie
e, Michael Chapin, Wheaton Chambers, Frank
son, Henry Brandon, Riley Hill, Sarah Hay-
Stanford Jolley, Harry Tyler, Effie Laird, Al-
Sessions, Noah Beery, Jr., Ann Kimbell.

SED WIRE (COLUMBIA) Producer, Armand
fer; Director, George Archainbaud; Screen-
by Gerald Geraghty. CAST: Gene Autry,
pion, Pat Buttram, Anne James, William Faw-
Leonard Penn, Michael Vallon, Terry Frost,
on Moore, Edwin Parker, Sandy Sanders.

ON GOLD (MONOGRAM) Producer, William
roidy; Director, Frank McDonald; Screenplay
/illiam Raynor; Based on James Oliver Cur-
's "Gold Hunters." CAST: Kirby Grant, Chi-
Martha Hyer, Frances Charles, James Farnell,
p Van Zandt, Harry Lauter, Moritz Hugo, Sam
Stanford Jolley.

T TRAIN FROM BOMBAY (COLUMBIA) Pro-
, Sam Katzman; Director, Fred F. Sears; Story
icreenplay by Robert Yale Libott. CAST: Jon
Christine Larson, Lisa Ferraday, Douglas R.
edy, Michael Fox, Donna Martell, Matthew
on, James Fairfax, Gregory Gay, Kenneth Ter-
Frederic Berest, Barry Brooks.

SEA TIGER (MONOGRAM) Producer, William F.
Broidy; Director, Frank McDonald; Screenplay by
Sam Roeca; Story by Charles Yerkow. CAST:
John Archer, Marguerite Chapman, Harry Lauter,
Ralph Sanford, Marvin Press, John Mylong, Mary
Corday, Paul McGuire, Lyle Talbot, Sam Flint,
Chad Mallory, John Reese.

CRIPPLE CREEK (COLUMBIA) Director, Ray Na-
zarro; Screenplay by Richard Schayer; Color by
Technicolor. CAST: George Montgomery, Karin
Booth, Jerome Courtland, William Bishop, Richard
Egan, Don Porter, John Dehner, Roy Roberts,
George Cleveland, Byron Foulger, Robert Bice,
Grandon Rhodes, Zon Murray, Peter Brocco, Cliff
Clark, Robert G. Anderson, Harry Cording, Cris
Alcaide.

SALLY AND SAINT ANNE (UNIVERSAL) Pro-
ducer, Leonard Goldstein; Director, Rudolph Mate;
Screenplay by James O'Hanlon and Herb Meadow;
Story by James O'Hanlon. CAST: Ann Blyth, Ed-
mund Gwenn, John McIntire, Palmer Lee, Hugh
O'Brian, Frances Bavier, Jack Kelly, Otto Hulett,
Kathleen Hughes, Lamont Johnson, King Donovan,
Robert Nichols, Alix Talton, George Mathews.

Dodsworth, Diana Douglas, Rex Reason in
"Storm Over Tibet"

Bert Arnold, Guy Madison, Gloria Saunders,
Ray Mala in
"Red Snow"

RM OVER TIBET (COLUMBIA) Producers,
Tors, Laslo Benedek; Director, Andrew Mar-
Screenplay by Ivan Tors and Sam Meyer;
ic by Arthur Honegger and Leith Stevens.
T: Rex Reason, Diana Douglas, Myron Healey,
ert Karnes, Strother Martin, Harold Fong,
ald Dyrenforth, Jarmila Marton, William Schal-
John Dodsworth, M. Concepcion.

AD MAN'S TRAIL (MONOGRAM) Producer,
ent M. Fennelly; Director, Lewis Collins;
enplay by Melville Shyer. CAST: Johnny Mack
vn, James Ellison, Barbara Allen, Stanford, Jol-
Lane Bradford, Gregg Barton, Terry Frost,
ard Avonde, Dale Van Sickle, Stanley Price.

RED SNOW (COLUMBIA) Producer-Director, Bo-
ris L. Petroff; Screenplay by Tom Hubbard and Or-
ville H. Hampton; Based on Story by Robert Peters.
CAST: Guy Madison, Ray Mala, Carole Mathews,
Gloria Saunders, Robert Peyton, John Bryant, Rich-
ard Vath, Philip Ahn, Tony Benroy, Gordon Barnes,
John Bleifer, Gene Roth, Muriel Maddox, Robert
Bice, Renny McEvoy, Bert Arnold, Richard Emory,
Richard Pinner, George Pembroke, Robert Carson,
William Fletcher, Richard Barron.

Massimo Serato, Maria Montez in
"The Thief Of Venice"

Keith Larsen, James Dobson, Marshall Thomp|
in "The Rose Bowl Story"

OLD OKLAHOMA PLAINS (REPUBLIC) Producer, Herbert J. Yates; Associate Producer, Edward J. White; Director, William Witney; Screenplay by Milton Raison; Story by Albert DeMond. CAST: Rex Allen, Koko, Slim Pickens, Elaine Edwards, Roy Barcroft, John Crawford, Joel Marston, Russell Hicks, Fred Graham, Stephen Chase, The Republic Rhythm Riders.

SECRET PEOPLE (LIPPERT) Producer, Sidney Cole; Director, Thorold Dickinson; Screenplay by Thorold Dickinson and Wolfgang Wilhelm. CAST: Valentina Cortesa, Serge Reggiani, Audrey Hepburn, Charles Goldner, Megs Jenkins, Irene Worth, Angela Fouldes, Reginald Tate, Norman Williams, Michael Shepley, Athene Seyler, Sydney Tafler, Geoffrey Hibbert, Hugo Schuster.

THE THIEF OF VENICE (20th CENTURY-FOX) Producer, Robert Haggiag; Director, John Brahm; Screenplay by Jesse L. Lasky, Jr.; Story by Michael Pertwee; Music by Alessandro Cicognini. CAST: Maria Montez, Paul Christian, Massimo Serato, Fay Marlowe, Aldo Silvani, Louis Saltamerenda, Guido Celano, Humbert Sacripanti, Camillo Pilotto, Ferinand Tamberlani, Liana Del Balzo, Paul Stoppa, Maria Tosi, Vinicio Sofia, Leon Renoir.

LADY IN THE IRON MASK (20th CENTU▮ FOX) Producers, Walter Wanger and Eug▮ Frenke; Director, Ralph Murphy; Screenplay Jack Pollexin and Aubrey Wisberg; Based on "▮ Three Musketeers"; Music by Dimitri Tiomkin; ▮ sented in Supercinecolor. CAST: Louis Hayw▮ Patricia Medina, Alan Hale, Jr., Judd Hold▮ Steve Brodie, John Sutton, Hal Gerard, L▮ Matthews.

PARK ROW (UNITED ARTISTS) Written, ▮ duced and Directed by Samuel Fuller; Assis▮ Director, Joseph Depew. CAST: Gene Evans, N▮ Welch, Bela Kovacs, Herbert Heyes, Tina R▮ George O'Hanlon, J. M. Kerrigan, Forrest Ta▮ Don Orlando, Neyle Morrow, Dick Elliott, St▮ Randall, Dee Pollock, Hal K. Dawson.

THE ROSE BOWL STORY (MONOGRAM) ▮ ducer, Richard Heermance; Director, William B▮ dine; Screenplay by Charles R. Marion; Color▮ Cinecolor. CAST: Marshall Thompson, Vera M▮ James Dobson, Keith Larsen, Richard Rober, Nat▮ Wood, Jim Backus, Ann Doran, Clarence K▮ William Forrest, Paul Bryar, Parc Launders, ▮ bara Woodell, Herb Vigran, Nancy Thorne, Sh▮ Ann Kelley, Anne Cottingham, Diana Dial, Car▮ Graves, Barbara Fisher.

Charles Irwin, Louis Hayward, Patricia Medina,
Sven Hugo Borg in
"Captain Pirate"

Cesar Romero, Marie Windsor, Rod Camero▮
"The Jungle"

CAPTAIN PIRATE (COLUMBIA) Producer, Harry Joe Brown; Director, Ralph Murphy; Screenplay by Robert Libott, Frank Burt, John Meredyth Lucas; Based on Novel by Rafael Sabatini; Music by George Duning; Color by Technicolor. CAST: Louis Hayward, Patricia Medina, John Sutton, Charles Irwin, George Givot, Rex Evans, Ted de Corsia, Malu Gatica, Sven Hugo Borg, Robert McNeely, Nina Koshetz, Lester Matthews, Sandro Giglio, Ian Wolfe, Jay Novello, Maurice Marsac, Genevieve Aumont, Mario Siletti, Robert Bice.

THUNDERING CARAVANS (REPUBLIC) Asso▮ ate Producer, Rudy Ralston; Director, Harry Kell▮ Screenplay by M. Coates Webster. CAST: Al▮ "Rocky" Lane, Eddy Waller, Black Jack, Mo▮ Knox, Roy Barcroft, Isabel Randolph, Rich▮ Crane, Bill Henry, Edward Clark, Pierre Watk▮ Stanley Andrews, Boyd "Red" Morgan.

THE JUNGLE (LIPPERT) Producer-Director, W▮ liam Berke; Screenplay by Carroll Young. CAS▮ Rod Cameron, Cesar Romero, Marie Windsor, S▮ ochana, M. N. Nambiar, David Abraham, Ram▮ rishna, Chitradevi.

Sterling Hayden, Ward Bond in
"Hellgate"

Phyllis Coates, Wild Bill Elliott, Myron Healey in
"Fargo"

GON TEAM (COLUMBIA) Producer, Armand
aefer; Director, George Archainbaud; Screen-
y by Gerald Geraghty. CAST: Gene Autry,
mpion, Pat Buttram, Gail Davis, Dick Jones,
don Jones, Harry Harvey, Henry Rowland,
rge J. Lewis, John Cason, Fred S. Martin, Fred
lson, Jerry Scoggins, Gregg Barton, Pierce Lyden,
lo Tricoli, Cass County Boys.

LLGATE (LIPPERT) Producer, John C. Cham-
1; Written and Directed by Charles Marquis
rren; Music by Paul Dunlap. CAST: Sterling
rden, Joan Leslie, Jim Arness, Ward Bond, Mar-
ll Bradford, Peter Coe, Richard Paxton, John
1ard, Pat Coleman, Bob Wilke, Richard Emory,
b Wooley, Kyle James, Rory Mallinson, Ed Mac-
, Timothy Carey, William Hamel, Stanley Price,
l Redwing.

UGHEST MAN IN ARIZONA (REPUBLIC) As-
ate Producer, Sidney Picker; Director, R. G.
ingsteen; Screenplay by John K. Butler; Trucolor
Consolidated; Music by R. Dale Butts. CAST:
ighn Monroe, Joan Leslie, Edgar Buchanan,
tor Jory, Jean Parker, Henry Morgan, Ian Mac-
1ald, Lee MacGregor, Diana Christian, Bobby
tt, Charlita, Nadene Ashdown, Francis Ford,
l Hurst.

FARGO (MONOGRAM) Producer, Vincent M. Fen-
nelly; Director, Lewis Collins; Story and Screen-
play by Jack DeWitt and Joseph Poland. CAST:
Wild Bill Elliott, Phyllis Coates, Jack Ingram,
Myron Healey, Bob Wilke, Terry Frost, Stanley An-
drews, Charles Space, Bob Bray, Denver Pyle,
Stanford Jolley, Stanley Price, Tim Ryan, Florence
Lake, House Peters, Jr.

TROPICAL HEAT WAVE (REPUBLIC) Associate
Producer, Sidney Picker; Director, R. G. Spring-
steen; Screenplay by Arthur T. Horman; Music by
Stanley Wilson. CAST: Estelita, Robert Hutton,
Grant Withers, Kristine Miller, Edwin Max, Lou
Lubin, Martin Garralaga, Earl Lee, Lennie Bremen,
Jack Kruschen.

THE RING (UNITED ARTISTS) Producers, Maurice, Frank and Herman King; Director, Kurt Neumann; Screenplay by Irving Shulman; Based on his
Novel. CAST: Gerald Mohr, Rita Moreno, Lalo
Rios, Robert Arthur, Robert Osterloh, Martin Garralaga, Jack Elam, Peter Brocco, Julia Montoya, Lil-
lian Molieri, Pepe Hern, Victor Millan, Tony Mar-
tinez, Ernie Chavez, Edward Siog, Robert Altuna,
Art Aragon.

e Murphy, Susan Cabot, Stephen McNally in
"Duel At Silver Creek"

Victor Jory, Vaughn Monroe in
"Toughest Man In Arizona"

HE KID FROM BROKEN GUN (COLUMBIA)
roducer, Colbert Clark; Director, Fred F. Sears;
creenplay by Barry Shipman and Ed Earl Repp.
:AST: Charles Starrett, Smiley Burnette, Jack
Iahoney, Angela Stevens, Tristram Coffin, Myron
Iealey, Helen Mowery, Mauritz Hugo, Edgar
Deering, Cris Alcaide, Pat O'Malley, John Cason.

THE DUEL AT SILVER CREEK (UNIVERSAL)
'roducer, Leonard Goldstein; Director, Don Siegel;
creenplay by Gerald Drayson Adams and Joseph
Ioffman; Story by Gerald Drayson Adams; Color
·y Technicolor. CAST: Audie Murphy, Faith Do-
nergue, Stephen McNally, Susan Cabot, Gerald
Iohr, Eugene Iglesias, James Anderson, George
Eldredge, Walter Sande, Lee Marvin.

FEUDIN' FOOLS (MONOGRAM) Producer, Jerry
Thomas; Director, William Beaudine; Screenplay by
Bert Lawrence and Tim Ryan. CAST: Leo Gorcey,
Huntz Hall, Dorothy Ford, Lyle Talbot, Benny
Baker, Anne Kimbell, Oliver Blake, Bernard Gorcey,
David Condon, Bennie Bartlett, Fuzzy Knight, Rob-
ert Easton, O. Z. Whitehead, Paul Wexler, Russell
Simpson, Leo "Ukie" Sherin, Arthur Space, Bob
Bray, Bob Keys.

Teresa Wright, Joseph Cotten in "The Steel Trap"

Paul Cavanagh, Sterling Hayden, Michael A in "The Golden Hawk"

ARMY BOUND (MONOGRAM) Producer, Ben Schwalb; Director, Paul Landres; Screenplay by Al Martin. CAST: Stanley Clements, Karen Sharpe, Steve Brodie, John Fontaine, Harry Hayden, Lela Bliss, Gil Stratton, Danny Welton, Mona Knox, Jean Dean, Louis Tomei, Joey Ray.

THE WAC FROM WALLA WALLA (REPUBLIC) Associate Producer, Sidney Picker; Director, William Witney; Screenplay by Arthur T. Horman. CAST: Judy Canova, Stephen Dunne, George Cleveland, June Vincent, Irene Ryan, Roy Barcroft, Allen Jenkins, George Chandler, Elizabeth Slifer, Thurston Hall, Sarah Spencer, Dick Wessel, Pattee Chapman, The Republic Rhythm Riders.

GUNS ALONG THE BORDER (MONOGRAM) Producer, Vincent M. Fennelly; Director, Lewis Collins; Screenplay by Joseph F. Poland. CAST: Johnny Mack Brown, Lee Roberts, Phyllis Coates, Hugh Prosser, Dennis Moore, Denver Pyle, Marshall Reed, Pierce Lyden, Stanley Price.

SCOTLAND YARD INSPECTOR (LIPPERT) Producer, Anthony Hinds; Director, Sam Newfield; Screenplay by Orville Hampton. CAST: Cesar Romero, Lois Maxwell, Bernadette O'Farrell, Geoffrey Keen, Campbell Singer, Alistair Hunter, Mary Mackenzie, Frank Birch, Wensley Pithey, Reed De Rouen, Lloyd Lamble, Peter Swanwick.

DESPERADOES' OUTPOST (REPUBLIC) Associate Producer, Rudy Ralston; Director, Philip Fo Screenplay by Arthur Orloff and Albert DeMor CAST: Allan "Rocky" Lane, Black Jack, Ed Waller, Roy Barcroft, Myron Healey, Lyle Talb Claudia Barrett, Lane Bradford, Lee Roberts, ward Cassidy, Charles Evans, Zon Murray, S Duncan.

THE GOLDEN HAWK (COLUMBIA) Produc Sam Katzman; Director, Sidney Salkow; Screenp by Robert E. Kent; Based on Novel by Frank Yer CAST: Rhonda Fleming, Sterling Hayden, Hele Carter, John Sutton, Paul Cavanagh, Michael / sara, Raymond Hatton, Alex Montoya, Poppy A. Vando, Albert Pollet, David Bond, Donna Mart Mary Munday.

FLAT TOP (MONOGRAM) Producer, Walter M isch; Director, Lesley Selander; Screenplay by St Fisher; Color by Cinecolor. CAST: Sterling H den, Richard Carlson, Keith Larson, William Phi John Bromfield, William Schallert, Todd Ka Dave Willock, Walter Coy, Clancy Cooper, Ja Best, Harlan Warde.

TROMBA, THE TIGER MAN (LIPPERT) Di tor, Helmut Weiss; Screenplay by Elizabeth Z merman and Helmut Weiss; Music by Adolf S mel. CAST: Rene Deltgen, Angelika Hauff, Gu Knuth, Hilde Weissner, Grethe Weiser, Gardy (nass, Adrian Hoven.

Arthur Franz, Frankie Lane, Eleanor Davis in "Rainbow 'Round My Shoulder"

Wayne Morris, Alan Hale, Jr., Lola Albrigl "Arctic Flight"

RAINBOW 'ROUND MY SHOULDER (COLUMBIA) Producer, Jonie Taps; Director, Richard Quine; Screenplay by Blake Edwards and Richard Quine. CAST: Frankie Laine, Billy Daniels, Charlotte Austin, Arthur Franz, Ida Moore, Lloyd Corrigan, Barbara Whiting, Ross Ford, Arthur Space, Frank Wilcox, Diane Garrett, Chester Marshall, Helen Wallace, Eleanore Davis, Eugene Baxter, Ken Garcia, Mira McKinney, Edythe Elliott, Jean Andren.

ARCTIC FLIGHT (MONOGRAM) Producer, L ley Parsons, Director, Lew Landers; Screenpl George Bricker and Robert Hill; Story by E Scott. CAST: Wayne Morris, Alan Hale, Jr., Albright, Tom Richards, Carol Thurston, Phil Arthur Garson, Kenneth McDonald, Paul Dale Van Sickle.

THE STEEL TRAP (20th CENTURY-FOX) ducer, Bert E. Friedlob; Written and Direct Andrew Stone; Music by Dimitri Tiomkin. C Joseph Cotten, Teresa Wright, Eddie Marr, Towne, Bill Hudson, Benny Burt, Joey Ray, Flint, Charlie Collins, Kurt Martell, Jonathan Stephanie King, Carleton Young, Katherine W Walter Sande, Tom Powers.

144

n Langan, Randolph Scott, Lee Marvin in
"Hangman's Knot"

Anthony Steel, Claudette Colbert in
"Outpost In Malaya"

RIZONS WEST (UNIVERSAL) Producer, Alfert
Cohen; Director, Budd Boetticher; Story and
enplay by Louis Stevens; Color by Technicolor.
T: Robert Ryan, Julia Adams, Rock Hudson,
McIntire, Judith Braun, Raymond Burr, Den-
Weaver, Frances Bavier, Rodolfo Acosta, Jim
ss, Tom Powers, John Hubbard, Walter Reed,
Monroe.

NGMAN'S KNOT (COLUMBIA) Producer,
y Joe Brown; Associate Producer, Randolph
t; Written and Directed by Roy Huggins; Color
Technicolor. CAST: Randolph Scott, Donna
l, Claude Jarman, Jr., Frank Faylen, Glenn
an, Richard Denning, Lee Marvin, Jeanette
n, Clem Bevans, Ray Teal, Guinn Williams,
e Blue, John Call, Reed Howes.

POST IN MALAYA (UNITED ARTISTS) Pro-
r, John Stafford; Director, Ken Annakin; Story
Screenplay by Peter Proud and Guy Elmes;
c by Allan Gray. CAST: Claudette Colbert;
Hawkins, Anthony Steel, Ram Gopal, Jeremy
ser, Tom Macauley, Helen Goss, Sonya Hana,
 Ho, Peter Asher, Shaym Bahadur, Bryan
man, Don Sharp, Maria Baillie, Bill Travers,
Stamp, John Martin, Myrette Morven, Patrick
wood, Alfie Bass, Victor Maddern, Yah Ming.

RIDE THE MAN DOWN (REPUBLIC) Associate
Producer-Director, Joseph Kane; Screenplay by Mary
McCall, Jr.; Based on Story by Luke Short; Tru-
color by Consolidated. CAST: Brian Donlevy, Rod
Cameron, Ella Raines, Forrest Tucker, Barbara
Britton, Chill Wills, J. Carrol Naish, Jim Davis,
Taylor Holmes, James Bell, Paul Fix, Al Caudebec,
Roydon Clark, Roy Barcroft, Douglas Kennedy,
Chris Pin Martin, Jack LaRue, Claire Carleton.

CATTLE TOWN (WARNER BROS.) Producer,
Bryan Foy; Director, Noel Smith; Screenplay by
Tom Blackburn; Music by William Lava. CAST:
Dennis Morgan, Philip Carey, Amanda Blake, Rita
Moreno, Paul Picerni, Ray Teal, Jay Novello,
George O'Hanlon, Bob Wilke, Sheb Wooley, Charles
Meredith, Merv Griffin, A. Guy Teague, Boyd
"Red" Morgan, Jack Kenney.

THE LADY WANTS MINK (REPUBLIC) Asso-
ciate Producer-Director, William A. Seiter; Screen-
play by Dane Lussier and Richard Alan Simmons;
Story by Leonard Neubauer and Lou Schor; Tru-
color by Consolidated. CAST: Dennis O'Keefe,
Ruth Hussey, Eve Arden, William Demarest, Gene
Lockhart, Hope Emerson, Hillary Brooke, Tommy
Rettig, Earl Robie, Mary Field, Isabel Randolph,
Thomas Browne Henry, Brad Johnson, Mara Corday.

Johnny Weissmuller in
"Voodoo Tiger"

John Derek, John Barrymore, Jr. in
"Thunderbirds"

WALKIE TALKIE (LIPPERT) Producer, Hal
, Jr.; Director, Fred L. Guiol; Music by Leon
in; Screenplay by Edward Seabrook and
 Carleton Brown. CAST: William Tracy,
awyer, Margia Dean, Russell Hicks, Robert
e, Frank Jenks, Alan Hale, Jr., Wong Artarne.

OO TIGER (COLUMBIA) Producer, Sam
an; Director, Spencer G. Bennet; Story and
play by Samuel Newman; Based on "Jungle
newspaper feature. CAST: Johnny Weiss-
, Jean Byron, James Seay, Jeanne Dean,
s Horvath, Robert Bray, Michael Fox, Rick
, John Cason, Paul Hoffman, Richard Kipling,
c Berest, William R. Klein, Alex Montoya,
.

THUNDERBIRDS (REPUBLIC) Associate Producer-
Director, John H. Auer; Screenplay by Mary C.
McCall, Jr.; Story by Kenneth Gamet; Music by
Victor Young. CAST: John Derek, John Barrymore, Jr., Mona Freeman, Gene Evans, Eileen
Christy, Ward Bond, Barton MacLane, Wally Cassell, Ben Cooper, Robert Neil, Slim Pickens, Armando Silvestre, Benny Baker, Norman Budd, Mae
Clarke, Sam McKim, Allene Roberts, Richard Simmons, Walter Reed, Suzanne Dalbert, Barbara Pep-
per, Pepe Hern, Victor Millan.

George Nader, Ursula Thiess in
"Monsoon"

John Boles, Gypsy Rose Lee, Paulette Goddar
"Babes In Bagdad"

BLUE CANADIAN ROCKIES (COLUMBIA) Producer, Armand Schaefer; Director, George Archainbaud; Screenplay by Gerald Geraghty. CAST: Gene Autry, Champion, Pat Buttram, Gail Davis, Carolina Cotton, Ross Ford, Tom London, Mauritz Hugo, Don Beddoe, Gene Roth, John Merton, David Garcia, Bob Woodward, W. C. Wilkerson, Cass County Boys.

GAMBLER AND THE LADY (LIPPERT) Producer, Anthony Hinds; Directors, Patrick Jenkins and Sam Newfield; Screenplay by Sam Newfield. CAST: Dane Clark, Kathleen Byron, Naomi Chance, Meredith Edwards, Anthony Forwood, Eric Pohlman, Enzo Coticchia, Julian Somers, Anthony Ireland, Thomas Gallagher, Max Bacon, Mona Washbourne, Jane Griffith, Richard Shaw, George Pastell, Martin Benson.

KANSAS CITY CONFIDENTIAL (UNITED ARTISTS) Producer, Edward Small; Director, Phil Karlson; Screenplay by George Bruce and Harry Essex; Story by Harold R. Green and Rowland Brown. CAST: John Payne, Coleen Gray, Preston Foster, Lee Van Cleef, Neville Brand, Jack Elam, Howard Negley, Mario Siletti, Dona Drake, Helen Kleeb, Vivi Janis, Ted Ryan, George Wallace, Don Orlando.

BABES IN BAGDAD (UNITED ARTISTS) Producers, Edward J. and Harry Lee Danziger; Director, Edgar G. Ulmer; Screenplay by Felix Feist an Joe Anson. CAST: Paulette Goddard, Gypsy Ro Lee, Richard Ney, John Boles, Thomas Gallaghe Sebastian Cabot, Macdonald Parke, Natalie Benes Hugh Dempster, Peter Bathurst.

HIRED GUNS (MONOGRAM) Producer, Vince M. Fennelly; Director, Thomas Carr; Screenplay Dan Ullman. CAST: Whip Wilson, Tommy Fa rell, Phyllis Coates, Henry Rowland, Stanford J ley, Dick Emory, Bob Wilke, Stanley Price, Hou Peters, Jr.

MONSOON (UNITED ARTISTS) Producer, Forre Judd; Director, Rodney Amateau; Screenplay Forrest Judd, David Robinson, Leonardo Bercovi Based on Play by Jean Anouilh; Music by Vasa Desai. CAST: Ursula Thiess, Diana Douglas, Geor Nader, Ellen Corby, Philip Stainton, Myron Heale Eric Pohlman.

ABBOTT AND COSTELLO MEET CAPTA KIDD (WARNER BROS.) Producer, Alex Gottli Director, Charles Lamont; Screenplay by Howa Dimsdale and John Grant. CAST: Bud Abbo Lou Costello, Charles Laughton, Hillary Broo Bill Shirley, Leif Erickson, Fran Warren.

Viveca Lindfors, Richard Conte in
"The Raiders"

THE RAIDERS (UNIVERSAL) Producer, William Alland; Director, Lesley Selander; Screenplay by Polly James and Lillie Hayward; Story by Lyn Crost Kennedy; Color by Technicolor. CAST: Richard Conte, Viveca Lindfors, Barbara Britton, Hugh O'Brian, Richard Martin, Palmer Lee, William Reynolds, William Bishop, Morris Ankrum, Dennis Weaver, Margaret Field, John Kellogg, Lane Bradford, Riley Hill, Neyle Morrow, Carlos Rivero, George Lewis, Francis MacDonald.

Charles Laughton, Lou Costello, Bud Abbo
"Abbot And Costello Meet Captain Kid

HIAWATHA (MONOGRAM) Producer, Wa Mirisch; Director, Kurt Neumann; Screenplay Ilona Vas; Color by Cinecolor. CAST: Vinc Edwards, Yvette Dugay, Keith Larsen, Eug Iglesias, Armando Silvestre, Michael Tolan, Rich Bartlett, Ian MacDonald, Michael Granger, Ro Bice, Katherine Emery, Morris Ankrum, Step Chase, Stuart Randall, Gene Peterson, Henry Cord

THE BIG NIGHT (UNITED ARTISTS) Produ Philip A. Waxman; Director, Joseph Losey; Scr play by Stanley Ellin and Joseph Losey; Based Novel by Stanley Ellis; Music by Lyn Mur CAST: John Barrymore, Jr., Preston Foster, H land Chamberlin, Howard St. John, Philip Bourn Emil Meyer, Dorothy Comingore, Joan Lor Mauri Lynn.

John Barrymore, Marlene Dietrich, Ben Turpin, Clara Bow, Robert Stack
PORTRAIT DOLLS OF FAMOUS FILM FOLK
By Mary Green, New York Artist, From the Daniel Blum Collection

Anna Magnani

JOSEPH BURSTYN)

WAYS OF LOVE

(Three Film Stories)

A DAY IN THE COUNTRY

Directed by Jean Renoir; From Story by Guy de Maupassant; Music by Cosma.

CAST

Henriette	Sylvia Bataille
M. Dufour	Gabrielle
Mme. Dufour	Jeanne Marken
Henry	Georges St. Saens
Anatole	Bordan
Rudolphe	Jacques Borel
Grandmother	Gabrielle Fontane
Innkeeper	Jean Renoir

JOFROI

Producer-Director, Marcel Pagnol; From Story by Jean Giano.

CAST

Jofroi	Vincent Scotto
His Wife Barbe	Annie Toinon
Priest	Tyrand
Fonse	Henri Poupon
Teacher	A. Robert
Antonin	C. Blavette
Marie	Odette Roger

THE MIRACLE

Producer-Director, Roberto Rossellini; Story by Federico Fellini; Screenplay by Roberto Rossellini and Tullio Pinelli; Music by Renzo Rossellini.

CAST

Nanni	Anna Magnani
The Stranger	Federico Fellini

Vincent Scotto, Henri Poupon
Center: Jacques Borel, Jeanne Marken
Top: Anna Magnani (center)

149

(REGINA-FILMSONOR)
UNDER THE PARIS SKY

Producers, Pierre O'Connell and Arys Nissotti; Directed and written by Julien Duvivier; Screenplay by Julien Duvivier and Rene Lefevre; Released by Discina International.

CAST

Denise Lambert	Brigitte Auber
Hermenault	Jean Brochard
Le Professeur	Rene Blancard
Milou	Paul Frankeur
Mathias	Raymond Hermantier
George Forestier	Daniel Ivernel
Marie-Therese	Christiane Lenier
Mme. Balthazar	Marcelle Praince
La Bourgeoise	Catherine Fonteney
Mlle. Perrier	Sylvie
Michel	Pierre Destailles
Colette	Marie-France

Brigitte Auber, Christiane Lenier

(DISCINA)
THE PERFECTIONIST

Producer, Andre Paulve; Director, Yves Ciampi; Screenplay by Yves Ciampi and Pierre Very; Adaptation by Pierre Very and Yves Ciampi; Music by Joseph Kosma.

CAST

The Chief	Pierre Fresnay
Florence	Renee Devillers
Tannard	Marcel Andre
Catherine	Claire Duhamel
Jacques	Roland Alexandre
Marcillac	J. C. Pascal
Gaston	Pierre Destailles
Jacqueline	Christiane Barry
Larmy	Michel Vadet
Yvette	Nadine Alari
Francois	Maurice Ronet
Albert	Serge Lecointe

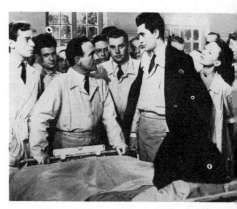

(Center) Pierre Fresnay, Roland Alexandre

(EALING STUDIOS)
SECRET PEOPLE

Producer, Sidney Cole; Director, Thorold Dickinson; Screenplay by Thorold Dickinson and Wolfgang Wilhelm; Assistant Director, Spike Priggen; Music by Roberto Gerhard; Choreography by Andree Howard; Released by Lippert Pictures.

CAST

Maria	Valentina Cortesa
Louis	Serge Reggiani
Nora	Audrey Hepburn
Anselmo	Charles Goldner
Penny	Megs Jenkins
Miss Jackson	Irene Worth
Nora as a child	Angela Fouldes
Inspector Eliot	Reginald Tate
Sgt. Newcome	Norman Williams
Pavillion Manager	Michael Shepley
Mrs. Kellick	Athene Seyler
Syd Burnett	Sydney Tafler
Steenie	Geoffrey Hibbert
Gen. Galbern	Hugo Schuster

Audrey Hepburn, Serge Reggiani

Willard Cele (right)

(SWAN FILMS)
THE PENNYWHISTLE BLUES*

Producer-Director, Donald Swanson; Screenplay by Ferdinand Webb, Donald Swanson and C. Pennington-Richards; Based on Story by James Brown; Music by Ralph Trewhela, Matome "Tommy" Ramokgopa; A Mayer-Kingsley Release.

CAST

The Thief	Tommy Ramokgopa
Lili	Dolly Rathebe
Mr. Shabalala	Harriet Qubeka
Lucas Ranku	David Mukwanazi
John	Victor Cwai
Mrs. Shabalala	Grnsell Nogauza
Isaac Wela	Lucas Khosa
Mrs. Wela	Linda Madikisa
The Priest	Jonathan Mzamo
The Pennywhistle Player	Willard Cele

*Original Title THE MAGIC GARDEN

Robert Cobo, Estela Inda

(ESTUDIOS CINEMATOGRAFICOS DEL TEPEYAC)
THE YOUNG AND THE DAMNED

Producer, Oscar Dancigers; Director, Luis Bunuel; Screenplay by Luis Bunuel and Luis Alcoriza; Music by Gustavo Pittaluga; A Mayer-Kingsley Release.

CAST

The Mother	Estela Inda
Pedro	Alfonso Mejia
Jaibo	Robert Cobo
The Lost Boy	Jesus Navarro
The Blind Man	Miguel Inclan
The Young Girl	Alma Fuentas
The Principal	Francisco Jambrino

te Etievant, Bourvil, Jacqueline Pagnol

(CLASSIC PICTURES)
THE PRIZE

Producer, Marcel Pagnol; Director, Jean Boyer; Screenplay and Dialogue by Marcel Pagnol; Music by Paul Misraki; Based on Story by Guy de Maupassant.

CAST

Isidore	Bourvil
The Mayor	Baconnet
The Priest	Duvaleix
The Doctor	Christian Lude
Brigadier of the Gendarmerie	Vilbert
Polyte	Jean Dunot
Madame Husson	Germaine Dermoz
The Young Girl	Jacqueline Pagnol
The Countess	Mireille Perrey
Virginie	Pauline Carton
Mlle. Cadenat	Suzanne Dehelly
Mme. de Gondreville	Nina Myral
Mme. Pitart	Jeanne Veniat
Marie	Yvette Etievant
Nicoline	Germaine Reuver

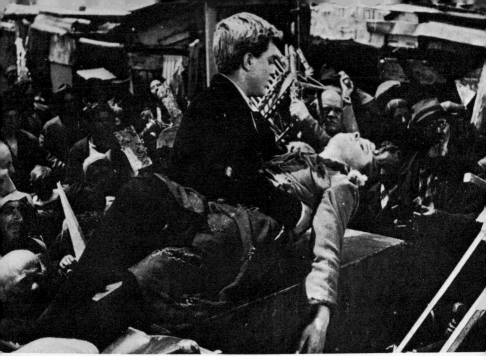

MIRACLE IN MILAN

Producer-Director, Vittorio De Sica; Screenplay and Story by Cesare Zavattini and Vittorio De Sica; Music by Alessandro Cicognini.

CAST

Little Toto (age 11)	Branduani Gianni
The Good Toto	Francesco Golisano
The Bad Rappi	Paolo Stoppa
The Old Lolatta	Emma Gramatica
The Rich Man	Guglielmo Barnabò
The Little Edvige	Brunella Bovo
Signora Altezzosa	Anna Carena
The Statue	Alba Arnova
The Unhappy Sweetheart	Flora Cambi
The Sergeant	Virgilio Riento
Alfredo	Auturo Bragaglia
Gaetano	Ermino Spalla
The Wrestler	Riccardo Bertazzolo
The First Commander	Angelo Prioli
The Second Commander	Francesco Rissone

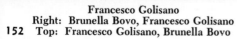

Francesco Golisano
Right: Brunella Bovo, Francesco Golisano
152 Top: Francesco Golisano, Brunella Bovo

(DAIEI)

RASHO-MON

Producer, Jingo Minoura; Director, Akira Kurosawa; Screenplay by Akira Kurosawa and Shinobu Hashimoto; Based on Novel "In The Forest" by Ryunosuke Akutagawa; Music by Takashi Matsuyama; An RKO release.

CAST

The Bandit	Toshiro Mifune
The Woman	Machiko Kyo
The Man	Masayuki Mori
The Firewood Dealer	Takashi Shimura
The Priest	Minoru Chiaki
The Commoner	Kichijiro Ueda
The Medium	Fumiko Homma
The Police	Daisuke Kato

Top: Toshiro Mifune, Machiko Kyo
Center: Machiko Kyo
Bottom: Machiko Kyo, Toshiro Mifune

Masayuki Mori, Machiko Kyo
Top: Kichihiro Ueda, Minoru Chiaki,
Takashi Shimura

153

(FAVORITE FILMS)

STREETS OF SORROW

Producer, Alberto Giacalone; Director, Ar
Gallea; Adaptation and Screenplay by Fu
Palmieri and Giorgio Pastina; Based on Book
Guido Cantini; Music by Alessandro Cicogni

CAST

Geraldine Brooks
Vittorio Gassmann
Franca Marzi
Saro Urzi
Lucille Marsh
Gemma Bolognesi
Bruma Danieli
Gianni Guarnieri
Armando Migliari
Carlo Romano
Aroldo Tieri
Viglione Borghese

**Lucille Marsh, Geraldine Brooks; Top: Geraldine
Brooks, Vittorio Gassmann, Lucille Marsh
Right: Geraldine Brooks, Vittorio Gassman**

(J. ARTHUR RANK)

THE IVORY HUNTERS

Producer, Michael Balcon; Director, Ha
Watt; Screenplay by W. P. Lipscomb, Ra
Mart, Leslie Norman; Story by Harry W
Music by Alan Rawsthorne; Color by Tech
color; Universal-International Release.

CAST

Robert Payton	Anthony S
Mary Payton	Dinah Sheri
Mannering	Harold Warren
Gwil Davies	Meredith Edw
Tim Payton	William Sin
M'Kwongwi	Orlando Mar
District Commissioner	Phillip Birkins
Chief Game Warden	Jack Arundel Mal
Watson	Kenneth Augustus Jer
Chief Veterinary Officer	
	Wallace Needham-C
1st Hunter	Edmund Stev
2nd Hunter	John Lawre
Ondego	Paul N
Kali	David O
Kimolo	Johanna K
Scarface	Jafeth Ana
Scarface's Brother	Bartholomew Sk

**Dinah Sheridan, Anthony Steel
Center: Anthony Steel; Right: Anthony Steel,
Dinah Sheridan, William Simons**

(...NCO-LONDON FILMS)

...EAUTY AND THE DEVIL

...ducer, Salvo D'Angelo; Director, Rene
 Screenplay by Rene Clair and Armand
...rou; Released by Arthur Davis Associates.

CAST

...Faust	Michel Simon
...isto	Michel Simon
... (Young Faust)	Gerard Philipe
...rerite	Nicole Besnard
...Princess	Simone Valere
...Prince	Carlo Ninchi
...mat	Tullio Carminati
...nt	Raymond Cordy
...y	Gaston Modot
...al	Paola Stoppa

Simone Valere, Gerard Philipe
Left: Nicole Besnard, Gerard Philipe

(...ZOLI-AMATO)

...OMORROW IS TOO LATE

...oducer, Giuseppe Amato; Director, Leonide
...uy; Story and Screenplay by Alfred Mach-
...and Leonide Moguy; Music by Alessandro
...gnini; A Joseph Burstyn Release.

CAST

...lla	Pier Angeli
...Landi	Vittorio De Sica
...Anna	Lois Maxwell
...co	Gino Leurini
...Directress	Gabrielle Dorziat
...lmaster	Armando Migliari
...or Giusti	Lauro Gazzolo
...ora Giusti	Olga Solbelli
...or Berardi	Carlo Romano
...ora Berardi	Ave Ninchi
...nina	Monique Van Vooren
...tant	Maria Giuseppina Ferrandi
...fina	Lina Marengo
...	Lucia Riccardo
...isto	Franco Nicotra
...ca	Patrizia Corsi Rota
...	Carlo Delle Piane
...retta	Eva Vanicsek
...o	Vito Chiari

Olga Solbelli, Pier Angeli, Gino Leurini
Center: Pier Angeli, Gino Leurini

(J. ARTHUR RANK)

THE MAGIC BOX

Producer, Ronald Neame; Director, John Boulting; Screenplay by Eric Ambler; Color by Technicolor; A Mayer-Kingsley Release.

CAST

Miss Tagg	Renee Asherson
Jack Carter	Richard Attenborough
Lord Beaverbrook	Robert Beatty
Father in Family Group	Edward Chapman
Graham Friese-Greene	John Charlesworth
Maurice Friese-Greene	John Howard Davies
Connaught Rooms Reporter	Michael Denison
William Friese-Greene	Robert Donat
Friese-Green Maid	Joan Dowling
Mrs. Collings	Mary Ellis
Elderly Viscountess	Marjorie Fielding
Maida Vale Doctor	Leo Genn
House Agent	Marius Goring
Mrs. Clare	Joyce Grenfell
Recruiting Sergeant	William Hartnell
Broker's Man	Stanley Holloway
1st Holborn Policeman	Jack Hulbert
May Jones	Glynis Johns
Pawnbroker	Mervyn Johns
Edith Friese-Greene	Margaret Johnston
Bath Doctor	Barry Jones
Warehouse Manager	Herbert Lomas
Bride's Mother, Wedding Group	Bessie Love
Orchestra Conductor	Miles Malleson
Sir Arthur Sullivan	Muir Mathieson
Old Gentleman, Bond St. Studio	A. E. Matthews
Cousin Alfred	Bernard Miles
Claude Friese-Greene	David Oake
2nd Holborn Policeman	Laurence Olivier
1st Platform Man, Connaught Rooms	Cecil Parker
Bridegroom's Father	Frank Pettingell
Arthur Collings	Eric Portman
Assistant in Bond St. Studio	Dennis Price
Mr. Lege	Michael Redgrave
Lady Pond	Margaret Rutherford
Helena Friese-Greene	Maria Schell
Ethel Friese-Greene	Janette Scott
Nursemaid	Sheila Sim
Soloist at Bath Concert	Oda Slobodskaya
William Fox Talbot	Basil Sydney
Earl, Bond St. Studio	Ernest Thesiger
Lady in Court Dress, Bond St. Studio	Sybil Thorndike
Assistant in Laboratory	David Tomlinson
John Rudge	Cecil Trouncer
Industry Man, Connaught Rooms	Peter Ustinov
Maurice Guttenberg	Frederick Valk
Hotel Receptionist	Kay Walsh
Doctor in Connaught Rooms	Norman Watson
Bank Manager	Emlyn Williams
Tom (workman at Lege & Co.)	Harcourt Williams

Right: Robert Donat, Laurence Olivier; Center: Robert Donat, Harcourt Williams, Michael Redgrave; Top: Robert Donat, Marie Schell

JOUR DE FETE
(THE BIG DAY)

Producer, Fred Orain; Director, Jacques Tati; Screenplay by Jacques Tati, Henri Marquet and Rene Wheeler; Music by Jean Yatove; English version by Borrah Minnevitch; A Mayer-Kingsley Release.

CAST

The Postman	Jacques Tati
The Circus Owner	Guy Decomble
The Circus Assistant	Paul Frankeur
The Old Lady	Santa Rellie
The Young Girl	Maine Vallee
The Barber	Rafal
The Cafe Owner	Beauvais
The Cinema Operator	Delcassan

and all the inhabitants of St. Severe-sur-Indre

Paul Frankeur, Jacques Tati, Guy Decom

156

(ARTHUR RANK)

THE IMPORTANCE OF
BEING EARNEST

oducer, Teddy Baird; Director, Anthony
th; Based on Play by Oscar Wilde; Music
enjamin Frankel; Color by Technicolor; A
ersal-International Release.

CAST

t Worthing	Michael Redgrave
	Richard Wattis
non Moncrieff	Michael Denison
	Walter Hudd
Bracknell	Edith Evans
dolen Fairfax	Joan Greenwood
y Cardew	Dorothy Tutin
Prism	Margaret Rutherford
n Chasuble	Miles Malleson
man	Aubrey Mather

: Edith Evans, Dorothy Tutin, Joan
wood, Michael Redgrave, Michael Deni-
Margaret Rutherford, Miles Malleson

Joan Greenwood, Michael Redgrave, Michael
Denison; Center: Michael Redgrave, Margaret
Rutherford; Top: Michael Redgrave, Dorothy
Tutin, Michael Denison

157

THE STRANGE ONES

Producer-Director, Jean-Pierre Melville; Adaptation by Jean Cocteau and Jean-Pierre Melville from Novel "Les Enfants Terribles" by Cocteau; Music by J. S. Bach and Vivaldi; A Mayer-Kingsley Release.

CAST

Elizabeth	Nicole Stephane
Paul	Edouard Dermithe
Agatha	Renee Cosima
Dargelos	Renee Cosima
Gerard	Jacques Bernard
Michael	Melvyn Martin
Uncle	Roger Gaillard
Maid	Jean-Marie Revel
Mother	Marie Cyliakus

and the voice of Jean Cocteau

Edouard Dermithe, Nicole Stephane

Top: Edouard Dermithe, Nicole Stephane, Jacques Bernard, Renee Cosima
Center: Edouard Dermithe, Nicole Stephane

(ARTHUR RANK)

ENCORE

roducer, Anthony Darnborough; Based on
ies by W. Somerset Maugham; A Paramount
ease; Music by Richard Addinsell.

HE ANT AND THE GRASSHOPPER

Director, Pat Jackson; Screenplay by T. E. B.
rke.

CAST

n Ramsey	Nigel Patrick
rge Ramsey	Roland Culver
da Ramsey	Alison Leggatt
Bateman	Charles Victor
ip Cronshaw	Peter Graves
Bateman	Margaret Withers
rude Wilmot	Margaret Vyner
etary	Dorothy Bramhall

WINTER CRUISE

Director, Anthony Pelissier; Screenplay by
ur Macrae.

CAST

s Reid	Kay Walsh
tain	Noel Purcell
tor	Ronald Squire
ineer	John Laurie
re	Jacques Francois
e	John Horsley
s Price	Joan Harben

GIGOLO AND GIGOLETTE

Director, Harold French; Screenplay by Eric
ler.

CAST

a Cotman	Glynis Johns
Cotman	Terence Morgan
ly Wescott	David Hutcheson
Espinal	Charles Goldner
a Penezzi	Mary Marrall
o Penezzi	Martin Miller
Barrett	Heather Thatcher
ian Prince	Guido Lorraine
an Countess	Daphne Barker

Nigel Patrick, Roland Culver; Center: Noel Purcell, Ronald Squire, Kay Walsh, John Horsley, John Laurie; Top: Terence Morgan, Glynis Johns, Mary Marrall, Martin Miller

Alec Guinness, Glynis Johns; Center (L. to R.): Alec
Guinness, Petula Clark; Alec Guinness, Gibb
McLaughlin; Top: Alec Guinness

(J. ARTHUR RANK)

THE PROMOTER

Producer, John Bryan; Director, Ron
Neame; Screenplay by Eric Ambler; Based
Novel by Arnold Bennett; Music by M
Mathieson; Universal-International Release.

CAST

Edward Henry (Denry) Machin	Alec Guin
Ruth Earp	Glynis Jo
The Countess of Chell	Valerie Hob
Nellie Cotterill	Petula C
Mr. Duncalf	Edward Chap
Mrs. Machin	Veronica Turl
Mr. Calvert	George Dev
Emery	Gibb McLaug
Police Superintendent	Frank Pettin
Mrs. Codleyn	Joan Hick
Bank Manager	Michael Horc
Mrs. Cotterill	Alison Leg
Shillitoe	Peter Co
Widow Hullins	Deirdre D
John	Harold Good
The Boatman	Lyn E
Yeomanry Officer	Michael Trubsh
Denry as a Baby	Paul Hop
Denry as a Boy	Matthew Guin
Joey the Mule	

160

(ARTHUR RANK)

THE MAN IN THE
WHITE SUIT

roducer, Michael Balcon; Director, Alex-
er Mackendrick; Screenplay by Roger Mac-
gall, John Dighton and Alexander Mackend-
; Music by Benjamin Frankel; A Universal-
rnational Release.

CAST

ey Stratton	Alec Guinness
hne Birnley	Joan Greenwood
a Birnley	Cecil Parker
nael Corland	Michael Gough
ohn Kierlaw	Ernest Thesiger
ford	Howard Marion-Crawford
kins	Henry Mollison
ha	Vida Hope
k	Patric Doonan
y	Duncan Lamont
kins	Harold Goodwin
Tailor	Miles Malleson
Watson	Edie Martin
lsen	Olaf Olsen
nering	Desmond Roberts
on	John Rudling
Lodger	George Benson

Alec Guinness, Joan Greenwood; Center: Alec
Guinness, Patric Doonan, Vida Hope; (left) John
Rudling; Top: Howard Marion-Crawford, Michael
Gough, Alec Guinness, Cecil Parker,
Ernest Thesiger

161

Joan Greenwood, Nigel Patrick

(ASSOCIATED BRITISH-PATHE LTD.)
YOUNG WIVES TALE

Producer, Victor Skutezky; Director, Henry Cass; Screenplay by Anne Burnaby; Based on Comedy by Ronald Jeans; Music by Philip Green; A Stratford Pictures Release.

CAST

Sabina	Joan Greenwood
Rodney	Nigel Patrick
Bruce	Derek Farr
Victor	Guy Middleton
Nurse Gallop	Athene Seyler
Mary Banning	Helen Cherry
Eve	Audrey Hepburn
Nurse Blott	Fabia Drake
Valentine	Anthony Deamer
Elizabeth	Carol James
Nurse	Irene Handl
Nurse	Joan Sanderson
Ayah	Selma Vaz Dias
Taxi Driver	Jack McNaughton
Man in Pub	Brian Oulton

Glynis Johns, David Niven

(J. ARTHUR RANK)
ISLAND RESCUE

Producer, Betty E. Box; Associate Producer, Peter Rogers; Director, Ralph Thomas; Screenplay by Nicholas Phipps; Story and Adaptation by Jerrard Tickell from his Novel; Music by Benjamin Frankel; A Universal-International Release.

CAST

Maj. Valentine Morland	David Niven
Nicola Fallaize	Glynis Johns
Capt. Weiss	George Coulouris
Provost	Barry Jones
Lionel Fallaize	Kenneth More
Trawler Langley	Noel Purcell
Brigadier	Bernard Lee
Georges	Jeremy Spenser
Sgt. Forbes	Patric Doonan
Sgt. Vogel	Martin Boddey
Kent	John Horsley
2nd Officer (Com. Ops.)	Michael Evans

Denis O'Dea, Vittorio Manunta

(SOUVAINE)
NEVER TAKE NO FOR AN ANSWER

Producer, Anthony Havelock-Allan; Directors, Maurice Cloche and Ralph Smart; Screenplay by Paul and Pauline Gallico; Based on Story by Paul Gallico.

CAST

Peppino	Vittorio Manunta
Violetta	The Donkey
Father Damico	Denis O'Dea
Strotti	Guido Celano
Father Superior	Nerio Bernardi
Monk at Door of Basilica	Harry Weedon
Old Workman	Edward Hitchcock
Doctor Bartolo	Frank Coulson
Sgt. of Carabiniere	Eliso della Vedova
Civilian Clerk	Alessandro Tasca
Chemist	Charles Borelli
Weaver	Mino Billi
Weaver's Wife	Gorella Gori
Guiseppe	Giorgio Riganti
Mrs. Strotti	Clelia Matania
Gianni	Robert Adamina

Robert Wagner

Zsa Zsa Gabor

Tab Hunter

Aldo Ray

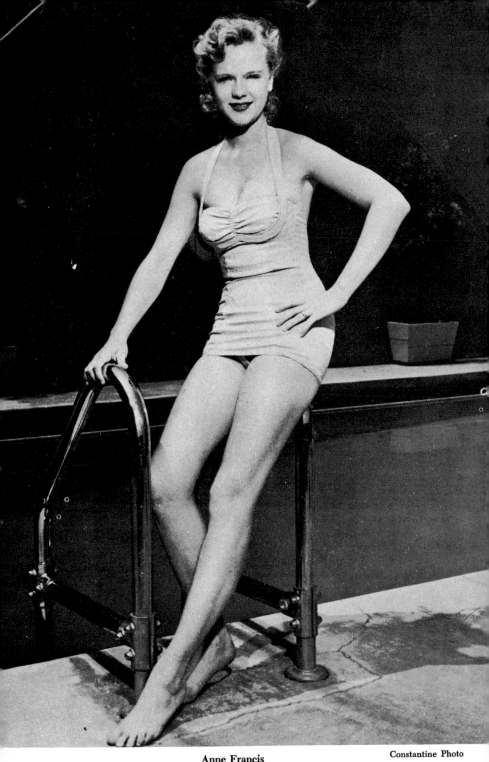

Anne Francis

Grace Kelly

Louis Melançon Photo

Dewey Martin

Constantine Photo

Jeffrey Hunter

Julia Adams

Keith Andes

Allyn McLerie

OBITUARIES

Julia Dean

Charles de Roche

John Garfield

RALPH BYRD, 43, film actor, died August 18, 1952, in Tarzana, California. He created the role of Dick Tracy on the screen. Among his many film appearances were "Jungle Book," "Moontide," "Stallion Road," "Canon City," "The Son of Monte Cristo," "The Penalty," "The Golden Fleecing," "Dark Streets of Cairo," "S. O. S. Tidal Wave," and "Mickey the Kid."

JACK CONWAY, 65, film director, died October 11, 1952, at his home in Pacific Palisades, California. He started in films as an actor with the old Nestor Film Company and in 1914 switched to directing. Among his more recent directorial jobs were "Saratoga," "Boom Town," "Viva Villa," "Tale of Two Cities," "Honky Tonk," "The Hucksters" and "Julia Misbehaves."

JULIA DEAN, 74, stage and screen actress, died in Hollywood, Octobert 17, 1952. She starred on the stage and in silent films for Universal in 1915. She retired from the stage in 1921, but in recent years has appeared in such films as "The Curse of the Cat People," "The Emperor Waltz," "Nightmare Alley," "Out of the Blue," "Elopement," "People Will Talk," "Easy Living," "Girls' School," "Experiment Perilous," "Do You Love Me," "Magic Town," and "You for Me."

CHARLES de ROCHE, 72, French actor and producer, died in Paris, February 2, 1952. His real name was de Rochefort. Paramount brought him to this country in the early twenties with the hope of replacing Valentino who was being difficult. Among his films were "Mon Homme" with Pola Negri, "Princess and the Clown," "The Marriage Maker," "The Law of the Lawless," "Madame Sans Gene," "Love and Glory" and "The White Moth." He also appeared as the Pharaoh in Cecil B. De Mille's "The Ten Commandments."

EDWARD ELLIS, 81, retired film and stage actor, died in Los Angeles, July 26, 1952. Among the films he appeared in were "Winterset," "Return of Peter Grimm," "The Land Consents," "Strictly Personal," "Fugitive from a Chain Gang" and his best known, "A Man to Remember."

WILLIAM FOX, 73, motion picture pioneer, died May 8, 1952, in New York. He entered the motion picture business in 1904 and in 1915 founded the old Fox Film Company. His early stars included Theda Bara, William Farnum, Annette Kellerman, Tom Mix and George Walsh. In 1935 the company merged and became Twentieth Century-Fox.

JOHN GARFIELD, 39, stage and screen star, died in New York, May 21, 1952. Under his real name, Jules Garfinkel, he became an actor with Eva Le Gallienne's Civic Repertory Company. In 1938 he changed his name and went to Hollywood. Among the films he appeared in were "Four Daughters," "Blackwell's Island," "They Made Me a Criminal," "Saturday's Children," "The Sea Wolf," "Out of the Fog," "Juarez," "Air Force," "Tortilla Flat," "Destination Tokyo," "Pride of the Marines," "Humoresque," "The Postman Always Rings Twice," "Gentlemen's Agreement," "The Breaking Point," "Under My Skin," "Body and Soul," "Force of Evil" and his last film, "He Ran All the Way." He was buried in Westchester Hills Cemetery, Mount Hope, N. Y.

HUGH HERBERT, 66, screen comedian, died March 12, 1952, at his home in San Fernando Valley, California. Among the films he appeared in were "The Great Waltz," "Little Accident," "Hello, Sucker," "Kismet," "Mrs. Wiggs of the Cabbage Patch," "Music for Millions," "A Midsummer Night's Dream," "The Perfect Specimen," "Tops of the Town," "That Man's Here Again" and "We Went to College."

GREGORY LA CAVA, 59, film producer and director, died March 1, 1952, at his home in Malibu Beach, California. He began his screen career in 1920 with Edison Films doing animated cartoons. Among the films he directed were "My Man Godfrey," "Primrose Path," "Unfinished Business," "Gabriel Over the White House," "The Affairs of Cellini," and "Living in a Big Way."

DIXIE LEE, 40, retired film actress and wife of Bing Crosby, died November 1, 1952, at the family home in Homby Hills, California. Among the films she appeared in were "Movietone Follies," "Why Leave Home?," "Harmony at Home," "Love in Bloom" and "Redheads on Parade."

ELMO LINCOLN, 63, film actor, died in Hollywood, June 27, 1952. His real name was Otto Elmo Linkenhelt. He was the original Tarzan of silent films and he played the character from 1918 until 1923. In 1949 he appeared in a Tarzan picture with Lex Barker. His last role was playing himself in "The Hollywood Story."

WALTER LONG, 70, pioneer film actor, died in Hollywood, July 4, 1952. He entered films in 1909 and was one of the best known villains of silent films. Perhaps his most noted role was that of the Negro soldier in "The Birth of a Nation."

J. FARRELL MacDONALD, 77, veteran film actor, died in Hollywood, August 2, 1952. He started his career with the old Biograph Company. He appeared in countless silent films for Imp, Triangle, Sennett, American and Pathe companies. Among his many films were "The Iron Horse," "Meet John Doe," "The Great Lie," "A Tree Grows in Brooklyn," "Nob Hill," "Johnny Angel," "Smoky" and his last role was in "Elopement."

HUGHIE MACK, 64, former film comic actor, died in Indianapolis, April 3, 1952. He was a comedian with the old Vitagraph Company in early silent films. In recent years he managed the Fox Theatre, an Indianapolis burlesque house.

RAY MALA, 46, screen actor, died in Hollywood, September 23, 1952. Born in Alaska of an American father and Eskimo mother, he made his screen bow in 1932 in "Igloo." He starred in 1934 in Metro's "Eskimo." His other films include "Last of the Pagans," "Call of the Yukon," "Mutiny on the Blackhawk," "Green Hell," "Zanzibar," "The Tuttles of Tahiti," and his last film this year, "Red Snow."

HATTIE McDANIEL, 57, screen actress, died in Hollywood, October 26, 1952. She appeared in over 300 films and won an Academy Award in 1940 for her portrayal of "Mammy" in "Gone With The Wind." It marked the first time a Negro performer had been cited by the Academy. Among her film appearances were "The Great Lie," "The Shopworn Angel," "Since You Went Away," "Maryland," "George Washington Slept Here," "The Little Colonel," "Judge Priest," "Saratoga" and "Nothing Sacred." She is buried in Rosedale Cemetery, Los Angeles.

POLLY MORAN, 68, famous film comedienne, died in Hollywood, January 24, 1952. Discovered in vaudeville in 1915 by Mack Sennett, she appeared in many of his early comedies. For a period she was co-starred with the late Marie Dressler in a series of comedies. Among her many films were "The Callahans and the Murphys," "Bringing Up Father," "Reducing," "Show People," "Hollywood Review," "Chasing Rainbows," "Rose Marie," "Caught Short," "Alice In Wonderland," "Prosperity" and "Ladies in Distress."

SUSAN PETERS, 31, screen actress, died October 23, 1952, in Visalia, California. In 1945 she was paralyzed from the waist down in a hunting accident and her recent roles were played in a wheelchair. Among her films were "Random Harvest," "Keep Your Powder Dry," "Assignment Brittainy," "Dear Barbara," "Song of Russia" and "The Sign of the Ram."

ALISON SKIPWORTH, 88, veteran stage and screen actress, died in New York, July 5, 1952. She came to Hollywood in 1930 from the stage and appeared in more than 100 films. Among them were "If I Had a Million," "Madame Racketeer," "Outward Bound," "Hitch Hike Lady," "Song of Songs," "Tonight Is Ours," "The Princess Comes Across," "The Captain Hates the Sea" and "Night Angel."

Hattie McDaniel

Polly Moran

Susan Peters

MALCOLM ST. CLAIR, 55, film director, died
Pasadena, California, June 1, 1952. He beg
working in films in 1919 for Mack Sennett. Amo
the many films he directed were "Gentlemen Pre
Blondes," "Fleet's In," "Canary Murder Case
"Montana Moon," "Big Noise" and "Bullfighters

FANNIE WARD, 80, actress, who starred in sile
films, died in New York on January 27, 195
Among the early motion pictures she appeared
for Lasky Film Company were "The Cheat," "Ma
riage of Kitty," "Tennessee's Pardner," "The Scho
For Husbands," "Common Clay," "The Yellc
Ticket" and "Innocent."

Fannie Ward

FORMER FAMOUS FILM FOLK

1902-1933	Adoree, Renee	1879-1950	Grauman, Sid	1879-1945	Nazimova, All
1883-1950	Allgood, Sara	1875-1948	Griffith, D. W.	1906-1948	Nolan, Mary
1887-1933	Arbuckle, Fatty			1894-1930	Normand, Ma
1868-1946	Arliss, George	1892-1950	Hale, Alan		
1896-1940	Ayres, Agnes	1900-1940	Hall, James	1880-1938	Oland, Warne
		1898-1948	Hammerstein, Elaine	1885-1942	Oliver, Edna
1880-1948	Baggot, King	1911-1937	Harlow, Jean		
1882-1942	Barrymore, John	1901-1944	Harris, Mildred	1893-1931	Phillips, Norm
1893-1951	Baxter, Warner	1894-1920	Harron, Robert	1896-1933	Pickford, Jack
1873-1928	Beban, George	1870-1940	Hart, William S.	1895-1936	Pickford, Lott
1883-1946	Beery Sr., Noah	1890-1942	Hawley, Ormi	1898-1937	Prevost, Marie
1881-1949	Beery, Wallace	1892-1950	Holmes, Helen	1873-1943	Price, Kate
1891-1932	Bennett, Belle	1907-1942	Holmes, Phillips		
1907-1947	Borden, Olive	1889-1951	Holt, Jack	1883-1946	Raimu
1867-1943	Bosworth, Hobart	1893-1943	Howard, Leslie	1891-1943	Ray, Charles
1893-1939	Brady, Alice	1893-1945	Hunter, Glenn	1892-1923	Reid, Wallace
1883-1950	Briscoe, Lottie	1884-1950	Huston, Walter	1861-1928	Roberts, Theo
1863-1915	Bunny, John			1865-1942	Robson, May
1902-1944	Busch, Mae	1882-1924	Ince, Thomas H.	1879-1935	Rogers, Will
1897-1946	Butterworth, Charles	1892-1950	Ingram, Rex	1893-1937	Roland, Ruth
				1898-1931	Rubens, Alma
1899-1936	Caprice, June	1887-1950	Jannings, Emil	1884-1929	Russell, Willia
1878-1947	Carey, Harry	1876-1916	Johnson, Arthur V.		
1883-1930	Chaney, Lon	1883-1950	Jolson, Al	1900-1919	Seymour, Clar
1887-1940	Clark, Marguerite	1892-1942	Jones, Buck	1882-1930	Sills, Milton
1885-1934	Cody, Lew			1863-1948	Smith, C. Aub
1872-1950	Costello, Maurice	1858-1929	Keenan, Frank	1888-1938	Stedman, Myr
1916-1944	Cregar, Laird	1880-1947	Kerrigan, J. Warren	1887-1939	Sterling, Ford
1884-1942	Cruze, James			1894-1941	Stonehouse, R
		1893-1917	La Badie, Florence	1899-1934	Tashman, Lily
1887-1934	Dane, Karl	1897-1925	La Marr, Barbara	1878-1938	Tearle, Conwa
1902-1950	De La Motte, Marguerite	1905-1948	Landi, Elissa	1898-1920	Thomas, Olive
1878-1949	Desmond, William	1919-1948	Landis, Carole	1905-1935	Todd, Thelma
1870-1941	Dexter, Elliott	1884-1944	Langdon, Harry	1878-1933	Torrence, Erne
1894-1949	Dix, Richard	1888-1938	Lawrence, Florence	1887-1946	Turner, Floren
1869-1934	Dressler, Marie	1887-1918	Lockwood, Harold	1874-1940	Turpin, Ben
1864-1920	Drew, Sidney	1909-1942	Lombard, Carole		
		1892-1947	Lubitsch, Ernst	1885-1926	Valentino, Rud
1884-1939	Fairbanks, Douglas			1894-1943	Veidt, Conrad
1876-1929	Farnum, Dustin	1892-1945	McGregor, Malcolm	1908-1944	Velez, Lupe
1880-1946	Fields, W. C.	1879-1936	Meighan, Thomas		
1869-1940	Finch, Flora	1882-1939	Mercer, Beryl	1894-1949	Walker, Johnny
1900-1951	Forbes, Ralph	1892-1940	Miller, Walter	1918-1951	Walker, Rober
1885-1939	Frederick, Pauline	1880-1940	Mix, Tom	1878-1936	Walthal, Henry
		1920-1951	Montez, Maria	1889-1938	White, Pearl
1897-1936	Gilbert, John	1902-1947	Moore, Grace	1866-1948	Whitty, Dame
1886-1948	Gordon, Vera	1886-1939	Moore, Owen	1895-1948	William, Warre
		1882-1938	Myers, Harry C.	1880-1927	Williams, Earle